Fisherman's Year

Fisherman's Year

The How, When and Where of Britain's Best Fishing

JOHN HOLDEN

The Crowood Press

First published in 1987 by
The Crowood Press
Ramsbury, Marlborough,
Wiltshire SN8 2HE

British Library Cataloguing in Publication Data
Holden, John, *1947–*
Fisherman's year.
1. Fishing–Great Britain
I. Title
799.1′2′0941   SH605

ISBN 1 85223 095 9

Typeset by
PCS Typesetting
Stoke House, Christchurch Street West,
Frome, Somerset BA11 1EB
Printed in Spain by
Graficromo s.a., Cordoba

Contents

Introduction

'All-rounder' used to be something of a derogatory term. In describing himself as not only an all-rounder but a pleasure angler as well, a man risked nothing less than ridicule, one implication being that anyone who enjoys himself on a wide range of waters, with fly, coarse and saltwater tackle, catching anything from dabs and eels to pike and brown trout, must be eccentric at least, and at worst some kind of freak.

Suddenly, it seems, a revolution is taking place. Adopting an across-the-board approach is regarded as an excellent philosophy, totally in keeping with the fast-moving pace of modern life-styles. Whether it be aimed at a single species like carp or towards the competition circuit, the specialist approach

Stillwater coarse fishing is widely available at low prices.

(Left) Described as 'the last stronghold of real fishing', the surf holds a fascination for all sea anglers.

will certainly continue to attract anglers at the top of the tree. For the vast majority, however, beginners and experienced alike, the decision *not* to put all their eggs in one basket becomes increasingly attractive. Meanwhile, the all-round approach encourages people to come into the sport who would otherwise not have made the effort.

Time and opportunity are precious commodities. It is all very well to dream of becoming a pike expert or a leading fly fisherman, but in reality very few anglers could ever afford the time and effort required – assuming they possessed the necessary talent and dedication anyway. On a mundane level, becoming a strictly freshwater, fly or sea angler also involves a fair amount of wasted effort; wasted, that is, in terms of hours or days spent waiting for something to turn up. It is a long, long time from one winter cod season to the next, for example, and the huge majority of cod beaches are dreadful places to fish during the summer. Eels and flat-fish apart, you're unlikely to catch anything.

Faced with the natural cycles of fish, the vagaries of weather and the restraints of family life, anglers who specialise are reconciled to spending a great deal of time preparing, surveying and generally setting the scene for relatively few periods with a rod in their hands, and yet fewer with a fish on the end of the line. Angling involves more than the act of catching fish, of

Sport for all: summer beach fishing is perfect for the family.

8

course, but there is always a balance of effort against results to be considered. For every one man prepared to spend months or even years in the quest for a 40lb pike, thousands would rather spread their time more thinly over pike, tench, trout and some sea fishing, the plan being to switch from one to another in step with peak periods in the species' annual cycle. On this basis, they can reasonably expect to catch fish all year round. Not only that, but there will still be a fair chance of latching into some specimens as well.

Fishing Cycles

No species of fish offers a consistent standard of sport throughout the year. Close seasons, inclement weather and personal opportunity aside, catch rate inevitably goes up and down as fish migrate, spawn, change feeding habits, grow lethargic or energetic in step with water temperature and air pressure – an open-ended list indeed. There is no fish so predictable that you can rely on catching it on a date chosen at random. The only way to be successful is to adopt the opposite approach of waiting for season and conditions to gel into a pattern which lends itself to good fishing.

A bass fisherman's ears prick up in spring or autumn when the wind blows

One man and his dog fishing the Norfolk Broads.

from the south-west or west and raises a moderate surf along the sandy beaches of the Atlantic coastline. He knows that without movement and colour in the water, bass won't come within casting range. In contrast, the zander fisherman heads for the bankside when a winter depression from the west or south-west pushes overcast skies and relatively warm air across the country. In this temporary break from winter's icy grip, the species may feed ravenously for a few days. On the other hand, in typical anticyclonic weather which blankets the country in blue skies and frost, he knows that the chances of catching a zander are virtually nil. Similarly, a bass angler understands why a sudden northerly wind in September will kill the surf stone dead. These ancient rhythms of cause and effect are fundamental to angling.

The result is that for long periods bass and zander fishermen, along with carp, perch, tope and any other specialist group, while away the time twiddling their thumbs and hoping for something to turn up. It is an attitude that

(Above) The ballan wrasse, probably the best target for the holiday sea angler casting a line from rocks and jetties.

(Right) Stillwater tench this size are a viable proposition for the all-rounder with limited opportunities.

more and more fishermen are unprepared to accept. Surely there must be something they can fish for today?

Such is the variety of angling in Britain that almost without exception an alternative does exist. Dreadful conditions for zander are excellent for flat-fish, whiting and sometimes cod as well. Still air and winter sunlight are absolutely marvellous out to sea, where you can catch cod after cod by boat casting a bunch of lugworms into the deep channels that cut between sandbanks. Conversely, when onshore winds force the boats to stay in port, local gravel pits and reservoirs might be excellent for pike.

The options and combinations are endless, but are available only if you ignore the traditional boundaries that restrict an angler to one branch of the sport. Some coarse anglers never dream of fishing in the sea or with a trout fly, often for reasons which even they don't understand. Fly and saltwater enthusiasts are equally blinkered into thinking that their speciality is the only one that exists. For a fast-growing section of the angling public, however, the barriers have come down. Being an all-rounder is back in fashion, and, due to our modern life-style, looks set to remain that way. The name of the game is to sample the cream of the fisherman's year wherever and whenever it can be found.

Making the Choice

Becoming an all-rounder is far easier for the raw beginner than for the established fisherman. First, a newcomer has no preconceived ideas to blur his judgement. Starting off with the express intention of dividing his time between sea, coarse and game fishing, he is never trapped by the usual constraints. Many anglers think that switching between disciplines is somehow wrong, or even an act of treachery; a stupid outlook, of course, but all too common. Second, there is tackle to be considered. Having spent a great deal on equipment for his particular type of work, the specimen hunter, matchman or beach angler is less inclined to start investing in more rods, reels and accessories. By contrast, the newcomer spreads his investment to create an all-round armoury which, although not as comprehensive as the specialist's, is more than capable of handling anything he may encounter during the fishing year. In fact, most experienced anglers are overstocked with tackle.

The decision to become an all-rounder can be made at any time. Begin by finding out what is available locally and nationally now and in the future, then plan a campaign with the intention of sampling as many kinds of waters, species, tactics and locations as can be conveniently packed into a full year. In-depth knowledge is of secondary importance to begin with. Angling is saturated with excellent technical guidance provided by tackle shops, clubs, books and magazines. Anything you need to know can be discovered very

Only a small river pike, but huge fun for the all-rounder.

Workmanlike tackle for all branches of fishing is relatively cheap. You do not need sophisticated rods and reels to catch lots of fish.

quickly indeed, whether it be tackle choice, bait preparation, fishing tactics or details of a good swim.

Without doubt, the best way to keep in touch with what is happening is to subscribe to a national weekly such as *Angling Times* and study the fishing column of your local newspaper. At the latest, catch reports are only ten days old so you can be sure that developing trends are spotted early enough for you to grab some of the action. A new trout fishery may open in a blaze of glory, or the cod might move in on a beach within easy reach, for example.

The feature pages of weeklies and monthlies are always geared to the changing seasons. From September onwards, expect to see plenty of how-to articles on pike and whiting; during May and early June, the spotlight will fall on carp, tench and match tactics for the new coarse fishing season opening on 16 June. It is all rather predictable for the expert, but makes essential reading for the newcomer and for those fairly experienced anglers hoping to spread their wings.

Clubs and Licences

These days many of the larger coarse fishing clubs offer open membership. Fill in a form and hand over the annual fee, and in return you are free to fish

in all their waters, details of which are updated and published at the beginning of each new season. Other than buying the mandatory water authority licence, which now normally covers trout and salmon, there are no formalities. Alternatively, go fishing in club or commercially managed day-ticket waters.

Trout fishing follows a similar pattern, being available on day ticket or on seasonal permit. It is now common for fishery owners to split the season ticket into three options: weekdays only, weekends only and all-in. Choose whichever suits your fishing calendar and pocket. For an all-rounder who can

(Left) The idyllic surroundings of a stillwater trout fishery.

(Above) A mixed bag of cod and bass from an inshore charter boat. Such fishing is available at very reasonable cost.

A commercial netter in the week, but a charter angling boat on Saturdays and Sundays, small inshore trawlers are a safe, economical way to get afloat.

never be sure what next week will bring, day tickets are probably the most economical option.

Beach fishing is free and generally unrestricted. Pier fishing is charged by the day or by the season. Boats are booked on a daily basis, the point to remember being that virtually all boats are chartered for a set fee which applies regardless of how many anglers go aboard. Standard practice is to divide the fee and bait charges by the number involved. Only a few skippers charge a flat fee per angler. It is therefore important to establish beforehand which system applies to the boat you have booked. Mistakes can be very expensive for a small group of anglers, and disastrous for the individual who does not understand the rules.

Tackle

A complete set of tackle covering all three main branches of the sport would be prohibitively expensive if bought at one time. Rods alone could total some £500. Reels and essential accessories would lift the outlay to around £1,000.

Where quality should never be compromised: cheap hooks must be avoided at all costs. These are of the finest kind.

Strictly for the enthusiast, an electronic bite alarm system with three sensor heads, widely used in freshwater specimen hunting.

(Above) Getting away from it all in the wilds of Scotland.

(Right) Two at a time – a fat whiting and a pouting from an autumn beach.

18

*(Above) Crucian carp:
unsung by the experts, it
still provides hours of superb
fishing for the pleasure
angler.*

*(Left) A catch to delight the
vast majority of fishermen.
To a specimen hunter,
however, carp of this size are
a waste of time.*

Fishing sounds an expensive game before baits, travel and fees are added.

The fact is, angling is quite an expensive sport in any case. Beach, boat and fly fishermen escape lightly, but their basic kit still totals over £300 when all the bits and pieces are included. At the other extreme, match fishing addicts may spend over £500 on one carbon pole and their overall outlay may exceed £2,000. By comparison, then, an all-rounder's outfit imposes no special financial burden. Built up over two or three years as he becomes more deeply involved, it usually turns out to be easier on the pocket than the figures alone might suggest.

The most logical plan is to build up a sound but basic outfit for each type of fishing in turn. During the first few years, most all-rounders concentrate on a handful of species and waters anyway. When a special rod or reel is required for what might turn out to be a one-off exercise, it can usually be borrowed. Buying new tackle under those circumstances is nonsensical, no matter how rich you might be.

Because the newcomer's initiation into the sport could involve any one of dozens or even hundreds of options in coarse, fly and sea fishing, it is imposs-ible to recommend the right tackle. Pick the type of fishing that most interests you or is easiest to locate, then ask someone who already does it to point out the right combination of rod, reel, line and terminal tackle. Tactics and baits are chosen on the same basis. For most newcomers, the local tackle dealer is the right man to approach. If he cannot help you directly, he will certainly point you towards somebody who will. All you have to do is ask.

Eventually, the rods and reels, hooks, lines and accessories build up until you find yourself the owner of a versatile range of gear capable of tackling all major branches of the sport. As a rough guide, your rod selection will include a 12-foot, 5–6oz beach caster, a 12-foot, 2–3lb test curve pike or carp rod (one model will probably handle both species), a lighter (about 1¼lb curve) rod of similar action for tench, a 13-foot fast action match rod and a reservoir fly rod between 9 and 10 feet for casting AFTM (American Fishing Tackle Manufacturers' Association) 8–10 lines. A keen boat angler will need either a boat caster or a conventional boat rod in the 20–30lb class. However, since these can be hired or are provided by the charter skipper anyway, the man who only occasionally fishes from boats has no pressing need to buy his own.

A small casting multiplier or surf casting fixed spool takes care of beach and uptide work, a medium capacity reel handles carp and pike, while a small fixed-spool or closed-face reel doubles for the tench-type and the match rod. Ideally it would be better to have a separate reel for each of the latter rods, but this is by no means essential. Finally, the trout rod needs its own specialist reel. The lines, floats, hooks and so on required for each type of fishing are best selected and bought as required. It is impossible to draw up a comprehen-sive shopping list. Even if it were possible, at least half the items would probably never be used. In all, the message is clear enough: buy nothing unless it is absolutely essential and cannot be borrowed. If you do buy, however, invest in high-quality products. Cheap tackle is always a waste of money.

Planning the Calendar

This book takes as its theme the continually changing pattern of angling as it is seen by the majority of fishermen. The options discussed are by no means comprehensive in the sense of covering every type of fishing and every species available in the British Isles. Salmon, sea trout, barbel and haddock, for example, are among the species not included, my justification being that the opportunities to catch them are relatively scarce and for most people would involve a considerable degree of pre-planning and travel – quite the opposite of what all-round pleasure fishing is about. Easily accessible sport is a cornerstone of success for anyone who must be economical with time and effort. The financial cost hardly comes into it; other than on the most exclusive river beats, salmon fishing is no dearer than top quality carp fishing.

The way to begin an all-round fishing career is slowly. Look around you and pick out the types of water and the species that interest you most. See how their peak seasons interlink with each other and also with your life-style. Then work out a simple calendar – don't make the mistake of overcrowding it – and get started. It really is as simple as that. Fishing of the quality and scope outlined in this book is there for the taking, probably closer to home than you ever imagined.

SPRING

1

Shore Fishing

Spring sees a switch of emphasis in sea fishing from the North Sea to the Atlantic coastline of England and Wales. It is impossible to predict exactly when the change will occur because so much depends on prevailing winds, currents and migratory patterns. Given a reasonably mild February with predominantly westerly or south-westerly winds, signs of renewed life are apparent by the end of March. By mid-April the season is in full swing, with the ray population well established in deep water, wrasse and pollack edging inshore towards the rocks, and a flurry of bass making their way in from the offshore overwintering grounds.

The split between east and west is distinct, but the exact point on the coastline at which it happens does alter from year to year, again because of the vagaries of weather and underwater environment. It occurs somewhere along the south coast, usually in the Solent/Portland Bill zone. To the east, summer fishing is definitely second-rate, while the farther you travel towards Cornwall and Wales, the better the prospects become in terms of species and overall fish population.

Flounders

Flounders are the most widely distributed of British flat-fish. Primarily an inshore species, they are smaller than their relative the plaice, extremely easy to catch, but none too popular for the table. Despite this, they play an important role in sea fishing; along with whiting, they are the very corner-stone of the sport. Probably more matches are won with flounders than any other shoreline species. For the pleasure angler, the non-stop action of a big shoal of hungry flatties is a highlight of the spring calendar.

Flounders spend much of their lives in tidal rivers. Highly tolerant of low salinity, they stray into the brackish water that permeates the head of estuaries. What they cannot do is spawn properly in such conditions, because the eggs and fry thrive only in high salinity. Consequently, from the New Year onwards, flounders migrate down the estuary system and out to sea. Full of spawn and permanently hungry, they are in peak physical and fighting condition.

Flounders can be hooked from virtually anywhere in the British Isles, but fish from Atlantic waters are the biggest and strongest. Whereas a good

(Above) An inshore flounder of typical size. Lots of fun to catch, but not very good to eat.

(Left) Surf rods and reels of 5–6oz handle all species from flounders upwards. The rod's power is essential for making long casts.

average east coast fish weighs about 12oz, fishermen in the west consider anything under the 1½lb mark unremarkable. 'Real' flounders weigh 2–3lb, and a handful over 3lb are reported most years. They make reasonably good eating as well, due to their relatively clean Atlantic habitat.

You can catch flounders on virtually any tackle capable of holding a bait on the sea-bed long enough for a fish to find it. In harbours and gently flowing estuaries fished at short range (most flounders are hooked within fifty yards of the bank), a pike or carp rod, 10lb line, 1–3oz of lead and a single flowing hook trace are an ideal combination. Even small fish fight well, yet the tackle is not outgunned by normal waves and currents. In rough conditions or at long range, a standard 5oz beach outfit rigged with a flowing trace or 2–3

A fat, clean-run flounder from the West of Britain.

(Right) Perfect Atlantic surf conditions with clean water, enough breeze to raise a surf, and plenty of blue sky.

hook paternoster is much more workmanlike, and virtually essential for serious match fishing where flounders are often beached two or three at a time. On the other hand, heavy gear overwhelms the fish and destroys its sporting appeal. What you don't have to worry about is delicacy of bait presentation: a hungry flounder takes absolutely no notice of hook size or line diameter.

Bait is a make-or-break factor, however. Essentially a predatory species, flounders prefer fresh meat. Strips of herring and mackerel, ragworms, harbour ragworms and peeler crabs are the classic baits. Squid usually doesn't work very well in numerical terms, but seems to single out the bigger specimens. Fresh frozen or live sand-eels are superb as well, ranking alongside peeler crab as *the* baits for western flatties. A chunk of bait the size of a thumb-nail threaded on to a medium or long shanked Aberdeen-type hook is about right.

Small-eyed Rays

Fishing for small-eyed rays can be a sticky business. First, the cold fear induced by peering down from the cliff tops to those sheer Atlantic rock platforms where the best sport lies. Later, the heart-popping, gut-wrenching sweat of toiling back up with a bag of trim little fish which sometimes swarm

Smaller and prettier than the thornback, the small-eyed ray has become a cult fish along the south and west coasts.

A rocky shoreline can be dangerous. Watch out for unexpected swells.

inshore during the warmer weather.

Having survived a small-eyed session or two with some of the more adventurous West Country, Welsh and Irish rock anglers, I claim no riotously overwhelming passion to make it a permanent fixture of my saltwater calendar. It is hard work, and downright scary on some marks if, like me, you were at the back of the queue when heads for heights were dished out. Small-eyed rays (some call them painted rays) hardly make it out of the featherweight class and don't scrap much harder than a sunken Sainsbury's bag, even on the rare occasions when they do make an effort. So why bother? In objective terms, I don't know. On the other hand, there is something about the sport that makes it worthwhile. You may find it mildly addictive without being able to put your finger on the reasons why.

Provided you use your head and take common-sense precautions, skipping up and down the rocks is not a hazardous occupation if you steer clear of the really mean sections. Do check with the local lads beforehand, however; some 'safe' marks are a lot more dangerous than they look, and many of the worst looking are actually smooth going. Bear in mind that there is a certain nonchalance about experienced rock anglers. Roughly translated, what they call 'simple' is just about manageable by a reasonably fit visitor.

So you're down on the rocks; what next? You could do a lot worse than tackle up a 5oz single hook paternoster or running trace, hitch on a lively sand-eel and toss out just beyond the rough stuff, preferably on to a patch of sand. This is not *the* way to catch small-eyed rays, but does offer a useful bonus for visiting fishermen with only a session or two to strike gold. Ray fishing is usually spasmodic, and this way you cover other options as well.

Any decent rock mark offers a reasonable chance of thornback, bass, flatties or even a conger or pollack, so even if you miss with the small-eyes, you won't go home fishless. On the minus side, the prospects for a really big bag of small-eyes are pretty slim, odd fish being the best to expect.

The main run of small-eyed rays prefer to stay in open water. Tackle sent whistling into the heavens so that it splashes down deep in the tide run generally intercepts not only more fish but bigger specimens as well. Traces stay the same as before – clipped for minimum air resistance if necessary – and baits include live and fresh frozen sand-eels, peeler crabs, ragworms and sometimes strips of absolutely fresh mackerel. 'Fresh' means mackerel feathered or spun on the spot, ideally sliced up and on the hook before the quivering has stopped. Whatever the bait, scale down the hook size from what you'd normally expect to use on big bass and thornbacks, for example. Small-eyed rays have modest jaws and tend to be nervous feeders. Needle-sharp medium-weight eyed hooks in the 2–2/0 range are ideal, tied to 15–20lb nylon.

Now scarce from the shore, the thornback is the tastiest and most highly regarded of the British ray family.

(Right) Digging ragworms from the estuary mud.

Tactics are very much wait-and-see. I've always done much better on reasonably small late evening and night tides with a puff of breeze tickling the water. A steady high, or rising barometric pressure is more productive than a falling glass, which in summer Atlantic regions usually precedes blustery weather coming in from the western quarter. Apart from any ill effect an onshore blow has on the rays, it usually prevents you from getting on to the best marks; even if you can, too much wind rules out extremely long casting.

Long casting from tricky rocks is tough enough at the best of times. Full pendulum-style is impossible, which explains the local preference for extended layback techniques and long rods. These days 13-foot rods are standard issue among the rock fishing army, simply because every inch of extra tip length adds vital yards to the cast. To increase range even more, leading exponents reduce their main line diameter to the equivalent of 8lb test or less. Cast from fixed spool, which is by far the better choice in this case, a 5oz rig running on 8lb monofil picks up at least twenty-five yards on the more conventional 12–15lb reel line. It sounds dangerously flimsy, but try it for yourself before you condemn it as impractical.

Surf Bass

Any fishing is better than no fishing, but surf casting tops the lot, in my book anyway. Clean oceanic water, white surf and a backdrop of sand and cliffs are a perfect setting. The tearing, savage jolt of a 6lb fish smashing into the sand-eel wriggling on your hook more than compensates for the uncomfortable days and nights spent waist-deep in the cold springtime Atlantic waters of Wales, Ireland or the West Country. Even greedy school fish are a treat.

Surf bassing is special, and that's a fact. However, it is not particularly difficult and you do not need specialist tackle. Light rods in the 2–4oz class are fun to fish with, but you can catch just as many bass, if not more, on a regular 5oz beach outfit. The option of casting to extreme range is a distinct bonus in spring, and shy-biting bass (another springtime characteristic) are much easier to hook if the bait is anchored by a grip-wired 5oz lead rather than dangled above a plain 2oz sinker which skids along the bottom when a fish attacks. Fairly heavy gear is a sensible conservation measure too, since fish are either cleanly missed or positively hooked in the jaws. Too many bass caught on light tackle end up hooked deep in the guts, from which they do not recover.

Timing and good bait are the secrets of surf bassing. Now and again the shoals react quite out of character and some lucky angler will hook a dozen fish from flat, calm water in bright sunshine. On average, though, the formula for real success is an onshore breeze, moderately high banks of breaking surf, clean water, no weed and overcast skies. Better still, fish at night. Within reason, the rougher it is, the higher are your chances of worthwhile sport. The

The combination of swell, surf and overcast skies attracts many shore species into casting range.

King ragworm on a fine wire hook lured this small school bass from the surf.

33

problem is knowing where to draw the line.

Bass switch off when too much sand and weed swirl in the breakers. Precisely how much they will accept seems to depend on location and season. I have taken a few bass in almost storm-force conditions when every cast produced a ton of weed. Sticking it out in the hope of picking up one big fish or a decent bag, however, is usually time and effort wasted. Steady, day-after-day surf is the stuff to concentrate on. If you must fish during stormy weather, pick the aftermath of a hard blow when the sea is dying down.

Local anglers who know their surf patterns inside out can predict bass movements and feeding times to within an hour or two. Planning a long-range trip to the surf beach is much more chancy. Unless you are in touch with the local grape-vine, the best bet is to watch the national weather forecast. Wait until a depression brings southerlies or south-westerlies, preferably

Bass move into deep water shore marks by the middle of April.

(Left) Classic surf casting country: Dingle Peninsula, Eire.

around the spring tide phase. All but a handful of Britain's premier surf beaches are on the Atlantic coast, so these are the winds that switch on the best sport. Rising winds that look set to blow for three or four days are a signal to load up and get going. The spring tide factor has no specific link with springtime itself, yet the heavier surge of water during those brief periods each side of a new and a full moon often livens up the sea and triggers the bass into a feeding spree. Equinox tides are a double bonus which virtually guarantee surf of some kind, and they mark the annual switch from winter to summer fishing trends.

Bait is the last piece of the jigsaw. For bait, read sand-eels. Surf bass will take lugworm, ragworm, crabs and fish baits, so if you get stuck this is a worthwhile menu to fall back upon. Whatever you do, though, get your hands on a boxful of live sand-eels. Rake or net them, or buy them if you must, but get them. Live eels outfish other baits about two fish to one; it is not at all uncommon to catch fish on eels when every other bait fails. I have tested sand-eels alongside lug (the traditional surf bass bait) on dozens of beaches from Devon to County Kerry, and the result is always the same. Oddly enough, very few beach men know one end of a sand-eel from the other.

A couple of dozen 6-inch sand-eels is plenty for a day's surfing. Store them in an icebox *without* water. Fish them on a 12 to 18-inch snood, paternoster-style, on a 1/0–3/0 long-shanked fine-wire hook – ideally a silver one. Thread the point and shank under the skin, starting at the tail, then clove hitch the nylon just above the hook around the eel's tail. Now pile on the casting power without stripping the hook.

2

Reservoir Trout

Fly fishing has a special something that generates enormous enthusiasm from anglers drawn from all walks of life. Unlike the best of chalk stream trout, salmon and sea trout fishing, it is neither exclusive nor outrageously expensive, and certainly holds none of the snobbish overtones that once deterred Mr Average from trying his hand with a fly rod. As time passes, the opposite becomes ever more true: modern reservoir and stillwater trout fishing is packaged and managed to provide a level of sport consistent with the angling public's limited aptitude and size of pocket. This does not mean that fishing is absolutely reliable and childishly simple. On the other hand, managers understand the need to ensure value, service and enough fish coming out of the water to keep the customers happy.

Thousands of reservoirs, lakes, gravel pits and the humblest of ponds are being turned into trout fisheries. Good fishing is available within easy reach of everyone, which is often far from the case with coarse and sea fishing.

Quality of fishing is maintained by restocking at regular intervals.

Indeed, some would say that there are probably too many trout fisheries. Whether they all remain financially viable is a question that only time will reveal, but meanwhile the result of commercial competition is a wide range of waters, prices and facilities from which to choose.

The big reservoirs like Grafham and Rutland provide plenty of space, fairly sophisticated bankside and boating facilities, reasonable stocks of fish and professional management in return for a modest investment on the angler's part. Mass-participation trout fishing began on waters such as these, and despite occasional hiccups they remain by far the most important section of the sport in terms of numbers of anglers and cash flow. For what it offers, the package is hard to beat.

Increasingly, however, anglers are turning to smaller, more exclusive and inevitably more expensive trout fishing in small to medium stillwaters ranging down from generous gravel pits to farm ponds. On either a day or season ticket you get more bank space, fewer anglers and, on average, a better

Rainbows of 1lb-plus are the basis of reservoir and stillwater trout fishing.

(Left) Small, exclusive stillwater fisheries stocked with big fish are increasingly popular with trout anglers willing to pay a little extra.

class of fish. All trout fisheries operate on a put-and-take system of some kind, but on smaller and more closely monitored waters it is easier for the owners to balance stocks, not only against catch levels, but also against the amount of money their clients are prepared to pay. One significant result is that in return for a slightly higher than average fee, most owners can afford to stock with trout much bigger than those ever likely to be provided on big public waters. A few actually specialise in stocking massive browns and rainbows grown almost to record size before being released.

Start of Season

Serious trout fishing begins in April when the banks are bare and chill winds cut across the water. Sometimes in early spring bank fishing is distinctly uncomfortable, and out in an open boat mere survival can be the angler's main priority. Despite the hardships, however, this is an excellent time to begin trout fishing.

The pattern of reservoir and stillwater trouting hinges on weather, ecological balance and the trout's habits. Most fisheries are heavily stocked prior to opening day with stew-bred trout that were brought up on food pellets. Never having hunted for themselves, they often respond to the splash of an angler's line, perhaps associating it with a handful of pellets. Bad presentation

Boat fishing in early spring can be uncomfortable unless you are properly kitted out.

might therefore actually pay off. Secondly, when trout are transferred into open water from stew ponds, they tend to remain in groups for several days. Again, this is good news for anglers, especially if they know exactly where on the bank stocking took place.

As the fish disperse and switch to natural foods, they generally head for deeper water because that is where small fish, insects and aquatic organisms spend the winter months. Although fly fishing in deep water with heavy lines may not appeal to the expert, it is technically easier for the beginner who still has to master the art of casting and presentation. Most fish fall to lures rather than flies, which again removes some technical pressure. In some respects, lure fishing is similar to spinning, and so calls for few of fly fishing's advanced skills and tactics.

In all, then, an early start allows time to familiarise yourself with the rudiments of the sport before late spring and summer bring fish up from the bottom to feed on hatching insects and other small creatures that live nearer the surface. In those circumstances, which will prevail throughout the rest of the season, the emphasis will swing more and more towards water-craft, fly selection and tackle control. In fact, during the height of summer, when the water lies mirror calm under blazing skies, trout are notoriously difficult to catch. To begin fishing then would be a sure recipe for disaster.

Learning to Catch Trout

Trout angling education is highly developed compared to what happens in the coarse and sea worlds. Virtually every fishery offers practical lessons on casting and fishing techniques, directly or through a local authority evening class. Private casting tuition for groups and individuals is readily available. Increasingly, practical tuition is combined with fishing theory and fly tying to give the beginner a complete overview of the sport, along with all the basic skills necessary for success. In addition, classes are an excellent means of breaking the ice, making new friends and generally coming to terms with the social fabric of a sport which for some curious reason still deters many would-be fishermen from making a start.

Fly Fishing Tackle

Another fly fishing myth concerns the price of tackle. Compared to any other branch of modern angling, fly fishing is usually far cheaper because apart from a rod, reel, line, landing-net and a few flies, hardly anything else is strictly necessary. Even today, a workmanlike basic outfit can be had for less than £100. Many beach and coarse fishermen expect to pay more than that for a rod alone.

Fly line weight is matched to fishing conditions. Here, a light line gives delicacy of presentation at short range.

(Above) Hooked neatly in the scissors, a rainbow trout shows its sharp teeth and powerful jaws.

(Right) Beautiful surroundings at Bayham Abbey, Kent.

42

Just as an expert beach angler selects a sinker and line before looking for a suitable rod, so the trout man must first identify which weight and taper of line suits his personal approach to the sport. This in turn is dictated by the waters he fishes, tactics employed and his physical strength. The only real difference between fly and any other kind of casting is that the fly line incorporates the casting weight instead of having it tied on the end in the form of lead or other dense metal.

Lines are identified by a code drawn up by the American Fishing Tackle Manufacturers' Association, and known as AFTMA or AFTM ratings. Line weight is expressed as a number – the higher, the heavier – and the taper and density are added as letter codes. An AFTM DT-9S, for example, is a 9-weight, double tapered sinking line. A standard line is 30–35 yards long, to be backed with about 100 yards of 20lb breaking strain nylon.

For long casting, heavier lines are generally best. Most reservoir anglers use forward taper (the weight is concentrated at the front of the line) or a shooting head, which is an exaggerated, higher performance type of forward taper made by splicing a short, heavy piece of fly line about 30 feet long to a backing length of thin braided or monofilament nylon. Short-range, delicate fishing is better handled by a double taper line whose weight is concentrated

Line and reel size are specified in accordance with AFTM rating figures. It is critically important that line weight matches the strength of the rod blank.

44

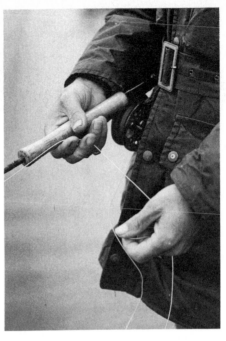

A strong rod and heavy line are necessary to achieve long casts from the bank.

Fly lines are retrieved by hand. The reel is little more than a storage drum.

A trout lure tied to imitate a small fish.

(Above) Casting platforms
enable a fly fisherman to
cover the margins of high
banks where casting would
normally be impossible.

(Below) Fly patterns reflect
the types of insects living in
or near the water. Others
imitate small fish, and some
are just flashy attractors.

(Above) Reservoir trout flies safely stored in a foam-lined box.

(Below) A rainbow trout coming to the net.

in the middle. Between these two extremes are all manner of tapers such as long belly and bug taper. Some are specialised, others are more fad or gimmick. Whatever the taper, floating, sinking and fast-sinking versions are available, chosen to match water depth and fishing techniques.

At the very least, the stillwater angler must have one sinker for lure and deep water fishing, plus a floater for surface techniques. From this baseline, rod selection is a straightforward matter of choosing a blank that matches the line weight, and whose length and action suit your physique and style. Regardless of all that is written about rod design, there really is little more to it than that. The reel? A fly reel is nothing more than a line store that plays no significant role in casting, fighting or retrieve. Provided that its capacity is sufficient, any reel of decent quality will suffice.

Fly Selection

It is said that flies catch more anglers than fish, a cynical view, perhaps, but one which highlights the difference between the relatively few patterns an

angler needs and the thousands more that hardly justify their existence as fish attractors pure and simple. In the long run, the best flies and lures for any given water tend to be drawn from a short list of universal favourites, backed up by those tied to suit the specific fishery in question. As such, they are best discovered by talking to experienced local fishermen and fishery managers.

Basically, the choice lies between dry and wet flies, nymphs and lures. With the exception of sedges, dry flies are not particularly important in stillwater fishing because of the ecological balance of the insect life. White Ghost moths and Daddy-long-legs are two likely to be required on the majority of waters. Traditional wet flies follow much the same trend. Most wet patterns have no direct link with a real insect – not necessarily a disadvantage in some areas of trout, salmon and sea trout fishing – but in the case of reservoirs and still-waters they in fact clash with the actual insect population. However, along with lures of all kinds (which represent small fish or attract by flashing, or simply by triggering a trout to attack through annoyance, frustration or as a reflex feeding action), wet flies are still useful and productive, especially when the trout are feeding on or close to the bottom.

Trout should be stored in a sunken bag, preferably of woven material. In hot weather, sealed plastic bags ruin a catch within minutes.

(Left) Trout tend to congregate where wind blows food into the margins.

Boat fishing reduces the need to cast long distances and might therefore be helpful for the raw beginner.

Still waters attract vast populations of chironomids or midges whose eggs hatch on the bottom into bloodworms, then metamorphose into buzzer pupae which swim towards the surface. Typically, they attach themselves to the underside of the surface layer, forming a carpet millions strong upon which fish feed. These, and other nymphal forms of insects, dominate the trout's menu and the angler's approach throughout the warmer months, and are therefore by far the most important factor in fly selection. Stillwater fly fishermen regard nymph fishing as *the* way to catch trout. For a handful of real enthusiasts it is the only technique to use; until season and conditions are right, they would rather not go fishing. Hundreds of tyings, colours and patterns have been devised, but the majority fall into only a handful of groups. Exactly which you need depends upon the water and the conditions. There is enough room there for discussion, argument and dogma, surely? On the other hand, many highly experienced trout anglers say that 90 per cent of the time a small, black buzzer imitation, fished with skill, is the deadliest killer of them all.

3

Boat Casting

Spring arrives many weeks earlier in the sea than on the land. By late February, water temperatures begin to rise along the offshore sandbanks and channels of the lower North Sea. Cod feed and travel through the region in large numbers, but there is a certain restlessness in the shoals. By mid-April at the latest most will be gone, leaving only a relatively small number of fish on the region's offshore wreck marks throughout the summer.

The thornback ray season begins as the cod fishing falls away. Sometimes the first rays arrive within range of the commercial and big charter boats by the end of February. Even after a winter so persistently cold that spring comes late, thornbacks will be there for the taking by March. During April and May, they come close enough inshore for small charter boats and dinghies to find them.

Tope arrive in the Essex area in late May and June. Swollen with pups, the big females are anything up to 20lb heavier than they will be later in the year,

A 20lb spring cod from deep water. For many boat anglers, a fish this heavy is a specimen never to be forgotten.

and consequently a real specimen in the 60–75lb class is on the cards for the dedicated angler and boat skipper willing to put in the time and effort to ambush the fish on their migratory routes through the channels of the outer Blackwater and Crouch estuary system. Fish in the 40–50lb bracket sometimes occur in plague-like numbers.

This annual cycle of cod, thornbacks and tope attracts anglers throughout Britain, and it is no exaggeration to say that during the spring period, the ports of Bradwell, Brightlingsea, Mersea and the Crouch are among the busiest in Britain. Not only are there fish to be had – and some really big ones as well – but, equally important, the style of fishing, called boat casting, is itself a great draw.

Boat casting is basically the same as beach fishing, but carried out from a boat. Rods are 9 to 10 feet long, balanced to cast 4–8oz, and matched with multiplier reels such as the ABU 6500 or Penn 970. The main line of 12–18lb nylon is headed by a shock leader strong enough to withstand the impact of hard casting. A simple overhead casting action produces distances in excess of seventy-five yards where necessary.

The principle of boat casting is to present the bait not under the hull or downtide of the stern as in traditional boat fishing, but at long range across the tide and, if possible, ahead of the boat and its anchor warp. The thinking

Charter craft range from old plodders to sleek offshore cruisers. On balance, a fast boat catches more fish because it has better access to the distant marks.

Charter rates apply to the boat regardless of how few anglers come aboard. Don't make the mistake of being caught for the whole fee yourself!

behind the technique is simple enough: fish in shallow sandbank waters and channels are wary of the noise and vibration pattern created by a moored boat, and will change path to avoid them. Therefore, the best way to catch them is to cast a bait beyond the disturbance. That the system really does follow such logic is demonstrated by fishing one rod traditionally and another by boat casting. The boat caster will catch between three and five times more fish.

Strong tidal currents are a feature of the best marks, and to a great extent they determine the terminal rig's design. The sinker must be fitted with wire spikes to anchor the tackle against the moving water, otherwise everyone's gear ends up in a bunch of knitted line astern. Sometimes a paternoster is the best way to present a bait or a series of baits, but for the most part a single running leger is far superior. Besides, when big cod, tope and rays are around, the last thing you need is two or three fish on the line at once.

The mechanics of boat casting involve a great deal more casting and fishing expertise than most beginners possess, so it is vital to go to sea armed with some idea of the basics of technique and in the company of other anglers and a skipper who know the ropes well enough to take you under their wings for the day. It is worth bearing in mind that all the help you need is freely available and generously given – you only have to ask. Most professional charter skippers will lend you the right rod and reel as well.

Don't take ordinary short boat rods and heavy reels. They are absolutely useless for catching fish; worse still, they are unfair to the rest of the anglers aboard. Apart from anything else, thick lines and big, plain sinkers so easily foul the flimsier boat casting equipment and also reduce the fishing space available in the boat.

Cod

Boat casting tactics catch cod from the species' first invasion of inshore waters in late October until the stragglers finally disappear in early April, but to my mind February and March are the most enjoyable times to be at sea. By then, bar the occasional cold snap or prolonged easterly blow, the weather is a little kinder with a hint of the warmer months to come. Bait-stealing whiting have gone and the run of cod themselves are a little bigger than before Christmas. Herrings and sprats with which the cod are preoccupied around the New Year have thinned out as well, which means you stand far more chance of hooking fish on baits anchored on the sea-bed. In all, the back end of the cod fisherman's year offers a perfect opportunity to sample the cream of the season, with a good head of 5–10lb fish and a fair sprinkling of between 15 and 20lb.

Finding cod in that offshore wilderness seems a daunting task for the uninitiated angler, but to an experienced skipper the pattern of surf on the sandbanks, the echo-sounder's print-out, and his familiarity with the way that the fishing has developed throughout the winter make locating the

Spring cod caught by boat casting from an inshore dinghy.

(Right) Waiting for a fish to grab a bait anchored at long range uptide of the boat.

The ultimate boat casting challenge – a 30lb cod hooked on light tackle.

shoals a reasonably predictable business. A good man will put you on top of fish three times out of four.

Sometimes the cod run in the channels between the sandbanks, and sometimes along the lower slopes of the bank itself. Exactly when and where depends on time, weather and the preferences of the fish in question. Whatever the case, fishing tactics are virtually the same: get a big bunch of lugworms well out from the boat, slightly uptide and anchored firmly on the bottom. That done, prop the rod against the gunwales with the reel clutch set to prevent the whole lot going overboard if a big fish grabs hold, and wait for the action.

Occasionally, cod pick up a bait so gently that the rod tip hardly moves. Mostly, they zoom in on the trace and grab the bait. The impetus of the attack rips the sinker's anchor wires from the sea-bed, and so the line falls slack. What you see is a sudden whack downwards of the rod tip followed by a rapid flick upwards as the tension disappears. Wind in the loose line until you feel the weight of the running fish, clamp down on the spool with your thumb and strike hard. Once the hook is set, the priority changes; the line must never go slack until the skipper runs the landing-net under your fish.

Thornback Rays

Thornbacks are the commonest species of our inshore rays, and despite continual commercial fishing manage to survive in reasonable numbers. Although they have declined in comparison with even ten years ago, the spring migration into shallow waters allows plenty of opportunities to catch what for many people is one of the tastiest fish in the sea.

Thornbacks visit the inshore sandbanks and gullies to mate and to lay their eggs among the sea-bed debris. Their annual pathways are not only remarkably consistent but interconnect with certain areas of the sea bottom – classically hillocks of sand and broken ground – where the shoals always congregate. Well known to netsmen and anglers, these hot spots are hammered unmercifully, yet somehow enough rays survive to provide next year's stock.

The name of the game is to locate a hot spot before a trawler moves in. Tactics are broadly similar to cod fishing, except that the mark is usually much shallower and undulating. The downtide slope of a sandbank is favoured because rays tend to lie there waiting to ambush food moving down in the current. A chunk of fresh mackerel or herring cast well away from the hull into the ray's larder stands an excellent chance of being attacked.

The bite of a thornback ray is virtually the opposite of a cod's. Initially, the rod merely trembles. Then a few inches of line click off against the reel's drag.

The 'skate' of the fish and chip trade is actually the thornback ray: ugly, slimy but tasty.

(Above) A fresh-run
thornback ray hooked on
herring bait from the
sandbanks.

(Right) A 50lb spring tope.
Had it been caught before
pupping, this same fish
might have topped 65lb.

More trembling and tugs spread over anything up to five minutes make you wonder whether a crab is chewing the bait or perhaps a chunk of weed has snagged on the line. Sometimes that really is the case, but if your bait is lying on the right spot, always give it a little more time. Suddenly the rod tip bends over and line runs steadily off the reel. Let ten yards go, then strike hard and maintain full pressure. As soon as you feel the dull, thudding weight of your thornback, lift her – most are females – away from the bottom and into mid-water where she will fight to a standstill. A 7–14lb fish on boat casting tackle in a big ebb tide is one of the highlights of the boat fisherman's year.

Tope

Half shark and half dogfish in many respects, the tope qualifies as the biggest predatory species likely to come the boat angler's way. Apart from true sharks and big conger eels, no other fish in British waters can challenge its combination of power and weight. In extremely shallow water, a tope is by far the fastest running species of fish that a British or Northern European angler will ever encounter. Although relatively shallow, the channels of east coast boat casting country are still a little too deep to drive the fish into turbo-boost when the hook sinks home. It is still a strong, demanding fish to control, however, rather like a heavyweight cod.

Tope are by no means confined to the east coast. Numbers elsewhere are almost certainly much higher, so that for a full year the catch figures of the Solent, West Country and Welsh ports, for example, put such spots as Bradwell and Brightlingsea into the shadows. However, the outer Thames and Blackwater boat casting marks outrank all others during the spring run beginning around mid-April and peaking in May and June. The proportion of 40lb-plus specimens is difficult to achieve elsewhere. Fish of 50 and 60lb, and the occasional monster topping 70lb, add a marvellous icing to the cake.

The earlier the fish arrive, the more chance you have of boating a record-breaker. Spring tope are heavy with young, and pupping begins in earnest as soon as the underwater nursery conditions are suitable. There is therefore a certain amount of luck involved in the capture of a fish topping the 60lb mark. Within days, that same tope will have lost anything up to 20lb to become just another respectable catch statistic.

There is absolutely no doubt that the odds of latching on to a really good tope depend on your finding the right skipper, and leaving it to him to choose the day. Men like John Rawle at Bradwell excel with tope because they are at sea all day, every day, and therefore know precisely when the packs of fish move into the area and what their movements are likely to be. The fisherman requires no particular skill other than the common sense to follow the skipper's suggestions of rig, bait and tactics.

These days, the majority of big fish are hooked on standard boat casting

Landing a tope by hand. Conservation-minded skippers refuse to use a gaff. Tope are returned after weighing.

tackle, a flowing trace reinforced with a short piece of wire to ward off the tope's teeth, and eel tail or fresh mackerel for bait. Surprising as it may seem, tope are not difficult to beat as long as you take your time and set the clutch correctly. A big fish can be a real handful, but except for the occasional monster that strips the reel in one unstoppable rush, the main risk is from failing to observe the two ground rules: small fish can be dragged protesting to the boat; big ones need coaxing.

SUMMER

4

Carp and Tench

Carp

The growth of carp fishing is nothing short of spectacular. Since Richard Walker and his contemporaries proved beyond all doubt that catching carp was a perfectly feasible exercise for any fishermen willing to devote to it the necessary effort, the sport has grown to dominate the freshwater specimen hunting scene in Britain and Europe. From June to October the hunt for big fish takes fishermen of all levels of dedication and expertise to the waterside. High technology prevails – boilie baits, electronic buzzers and long-range casting rods are standard weapons in the quest for more and bigger fish.

Over 30lb is the important target weight for most carp men. Although a 20lb fish would never be despised, it is increasingly regarded as just one more step along the road to the magic 50lb mark. Some experts number their

Common carp caught from a tench swim.

*Crucians are not considered
to be part of the 'real' carp
world.*

*Carp specialists use high-
power catapults to bait
distant swims.*

season's toll of specimens over 20lb in dozens; a few achieve the century.

To concentrate on big fish ignores the potential of smaller carp to provide endless pleasure and opportunity for thousands of freshwater fishermen who are unable or unwilling to commit themselves completely to the rarefied atmosphere of top-class specimen hunting. In truth, he is a pessimistic angler indeed who rates carp in the 5–15lb range as unworthy of his time and skills. For most anglers, such a fish may well be the catch of a lifetime.

This fundamental split between pleasure fishing and outright specialisation should be seen in perspective. To the outsider it seems that the upper levels of the carp world grow more jealous of each other's achievements and become ridiculously secretive about tackle, baits and waters. They see it all as part of the game, but for 99 per cent of coarse fishermen it is the signal to switch off. Where is the fun in it? For the all-rounder, fishing is as much about fun as about catching fish. If you don't like it, why bother going? The spin-off question is, can carp fishing still be successful when attempted in a lighter vein, or is it an all-or-nothing exercise? The answer is a resounding yes, you can be fairly relaxed in your approach yet still catch plenty of fish – including some big ones.

Carp Fisheries

Revolutionary tackle and techniques are not the sole reason why so many more fish are caught these days. Carp fishing is close to being in a contrived situation; regular stocking and continual supply of artificial food, courtesy of anglers who throw in literally thousands of attractors and hook baits, have become fundamental to the development of the sport. A disinterested observer may even conclude that the majority of waters are artificially programmed for the benefit of the anglers concerned. In the sense that excellent carp fishing is readily available throughout most of Britain, that is certainly close to the truth. It does not mean that skill is no longer required, however. Big fish are still more difficult to catch, and probably always will be.

The good news for all-round fishermen is that with every passing season, more and more carp fishing is available on club and day-ticket waters. Since most waters are predominantly stocked with small fish, ponds, lakes and gravel pits with a good head of carp in the 5–15lb band are fast becoming a universal feature of British coarse angling. Many clubs and commercially run fisheries also supplement their basic stocks with a few big fish in the 20lb class in order to cater for the specialists. It is also a good business ploy, as anglers willingly pay more when they have the chance of hooking a monster. A carp over 30lb ensures any water a place on the specimen hunting circuit.

Returning a big carp. Catching the same fish time after time is a common occurrence on heavily fished waters.

(Right) A 10lb common carp landed on match tackle baited with a single caster.

Carp Fishing Options

Common, leather and mirror carp are variations of the same fish. With the exception of a few stray imported species like the grass carp, the only other species of interest to anglers is the crucian carp. Far smaller and less widespread, it has no real link with the world of serious carp fishing.

Reference has already been made to the gulf between specimen hunting and pleasure fishing. This is paralleled by differences between the techniques involved in setting out to catch lots of smallish fish or sticking it out for days, weeks or even years for just one monster carp. From the practical point of view, a great deal hinges on the feeding habits and life-style of big fish compared to small ones. In some ways they can be considered as two distinct species, because what works with one group will not give you the best chance with the other. For the non-specialist angler hoping to put carp on the bank, this is a fundamental piece of the puzzle.

Although getting on for double figures, this common carp caught by England match star Bob Nudd fell to light float tackle.

Far from what you would expect carp tackle to be: match rod, light line, size 18 hook and a float. However, that is what it takes to catch carp on this heavily match-fished water.

A 2–2½lb test curve rod is essential for landing big carp. The same power might well be required to cast baits a hundred yards or more.

(Above) Two 'twenties' for carp expert Del Romang.

(Right) The carp angler's dream.

Smaller Carp

Carp, like all fish, adapt themselves to the environment they happen to find themselves in. To a greater extent than probably any other fish, they match their feeding habits to what anglers throw in, regardless of whether the hook baits or ground baits are actually intended for the species.

A fine example is where large numbers of fairly small carp are introduced into a heavily match-fished water. Before long, they develop a reflex reaction to the splash of bait and tackle. A few balls of ground bait are a signal for every carp in the water to descend on the area. Similarly, they soon learn that loose-fed casters rise to the surface, then drift along the wind lanes. In the evening after the matchmen have gone, the reeded margins are alive with carp mopping up the last of the day's free offerings.

Successful tactics take advantage of that learned response. The idea of taking carp over 5lb on a single caster fished on a 1½lb breaking strain hook link may sound ridiculous, but it could prove to be the supreme technique for such a water. Similarly, where carp have been weaned on to baits and techniques meant for roach, bream, tench and other smaller species, these feeding patterns should be taken into consideration when you plan a campaign.

A small common carp preoccupied with feeding on casters and other match baits. Such fish are commonplace these days.

Big Fish

On most waters with a mixed carp population, the life-style of a big fish is more in keeping with the species' natural habits. Fish in the 10–15lb range tend to live in small groups; above 20lb, the urge to be solitary is ever stronger. Big fish also maintain feeding habits more aligned to a truly wild fish. Essentially they are bottom feeders, not unlike an underwater equivalent of the pig. They also feed at the surface and search along the margins, but the extent to which they do so depends on how much food is available there – which in turn reflects how much floating or semi-buoyant bait is discarded or deliberately introduced by anglers.

Wild fish eat what nature provides, but in today's carp waters their diet is strongly biased towards the nutrients and flavourings of the carp angler's boilies, plus the various particle baits. Only a few carp anglers still prefer potatoes, bread and similar traditional baits. So much bait goes into the average water during the season that there can be no doubt that it becomes an important – probably the dominant – food source. Herein lies the key to successful angling: the fish are almost exclusively preoccupied with scavenging through a carpet of free offerings, so the best way to hook one is to pre-bait a swim of your own, then leger a particle or boilie.

In principle, carp fishing is no more difficult than that. The mechanics of the sport are only a small part of the overall picture, however. Real success demands a great deal of observation to isolate the right swims and identify the carp's movements and timetable. This alone may take months to establish. Next comes the sometimes slow business of gradually weaning the fish on to a suitable bait mix and flavouring combination. It is generally accepted by carp experts that fish do learn to distinguish between additives and flavourings. Having been hooked on one type, they may refuse it in future and may take several weeks to accept a new one. In all, then, this water analysis and pre-conditioning of feeding pattern calls for a high level of involvement and dedication. Whether it is worth while for the all-rounder to become so devoted to a single species is a question that only he can answer.

Tench

The carp fishing boom is not everyone's idea of fun. When a public or club water comes under heavy pressure from bivvies and boilies, the non-carp anglers often find themselves squeezed out of popular swims and forced to switch angling tactics as well. Excessive baiting alters the feeding habits of other species until they become very difficult to catch by more conventional methods and baits.

For these and a hundred more reasons, the majority of anglers who fish as much for relaxation as anything, but still intend to make good catches, are

(Above) The full specimen hunting set-up, with three carbon-fibre rods, matched reels and an electronic buzzer alarm system.

(Left) Returning a fish to its home among the underwater roots.

(Right) Some traditionalist anglers value tench more highly than carp.

74

beginning to turn their attention to other species. Tench are close to the top of the list. Widely distributed, able to thrive in stillwaters of all kinds, including those with the fairly high silt levels characteristic of middle-aged gravel pits, wily and strong enough to test man and tackle, the tench is an ideal candidate for pleasure and specialist angler alike.

The tench has always been among the freshwater angler's favourite species. For centuries it has been regarded as the archetypal fish of summer dawn. Rising mist, calm water and streams of tiny bubbles around the float as it lies alongside lily pads is a picture dear to the hearts of anglers past, present and future. Yet classic tenching has been so overshadowed by the more strident and technical world of carp fishing that there must be thousands of fishermen who have never sampled the magic spell that only the tench can weave. The signs are that change is on the way, with the species set to make a big come-back.

Tench and carp do not have a particularly friendly relationship under the best of circumstances, and are often at loggerheads. Sometimes one species – usually the carp – becomes dominant and pushes the other into decline. More

A magic moment for the night fisherman as a fish picks up his bait.

often, though, they live under a reasonably amicable truce. Tench and carp zones dovetail into each other like an underwater jigsaw, so it is quite possible to catch both from the same pitch provided that you cast your bait into the appropriate place. Carp may patrol along a channel at the far end of the swim beneath overhanging branches, for instance, while a shoal of tench feeds on a muddy bottom almost below the rod tip.

Bloodworms and other aquatic animals make up the bulk of the tench's natural diet. Muddy bottoms are therefore a prominent feature of good tench swims; the bubble patterns that indicate the presence of a feeding shoal are probably produced by a combination of trapped gases rising to the surface as the tench forages and its habit of using gills and mouth as an underwater vacuum cleaner.

This normal system of foraging along the bottom gives a clue to successful baits: worms, maggots and bread flake are traditional favourites which tench will readily accept after only a limited amount of pre-baiting. Raking the swim bottom also encourages them to feed, for obvious reasons.

These approaches still work well in many waters but the effectiveness is increasingly influenced by modern tactics aimed chiefly at carp. The vast numbers of boilie and particle baits fed into stillwaters for the carp's benefit inevitably attract other species. The tench is encouraged to switch to them because of its bottom feeding habits. In the short term it means that tench are more easily caught on scaled down carp baits and particles like sweetcorn than on the traditional baits.

Over a period, the availability of vast amounts of concentrated protein might well explain the upsurge in big tench. Tench above the 8lb mark are almost a reasonable target for the dedicated specialist angler, whereas ten years ago they were regarded as an impossible dream. Average weights have risen across the board as well, with excellent fish in the 3–5lb category becoming quite common on many waters. Whatever the pros and cons of artificial feeding may be, this is certainly good news for the non-specialist fisherman hoping to enjoy a superb day's sport without having to work all season in preparation.

Tench Tactics

Tench techniques are dictated by the overall angling pattern of the water involved. Where fish still rely on natural food and non-specialist baits like maggots and bread, the conventional system of ground baiting the swim, then fishing with float or lift leger tackle, is both productive and sporting and has the distinct advantage of laying a framework for species other than tench. Bream and roach may turn up instead, or as part of a mixed bag. For the all-rounder such options are considered to be icing on the cake, not least because his time is usually limited.

A pair of big tench landed by specimen hunter Dave Plummer.

(Left) The Master at work. Len Head, acknowledged as one of Europe's leading tench fishermen, with a bag of fish up to 6lb caught in a single session.

Where tench are preoccupied on carp-type baits, mini boilies and particles hold the key to consistent success. If the water has been hammered particularly hard, hair rigs and exotically flavoured bait mixes might become absolutely essential for the capture of all but the smallest of tench. Along with that change in feeding preferences comes greater caution, increased fussiness and a general break up of the life-style that could be expected if the tench were left to their own devices. Sometimes the angler needs to think in terms of carp rather than tench, even though the latter species is his real target. Certainly it is a philosophy that produces huge fish, but is it proper tench fishing? According to the growing voice of discontent in non-specialist circles, it is a backwards step which should be corrected without delay.

5

Sea Angling from Rocks and Harbours

By June, summer species are strongly established in the deep water close to rocks, jetties and harbour walls. Making the distinction between these deep marks and the coastline in general is essential because the day to day pattern of fishing in shallow water is very different, due to clarity, disturbance and the tidal rhythm. The fish population of, for example, a storm beach is always transitory and therefore unpredictable, calling for a lot of effort and skill to produce even modest results. During the holiday season, many anglers cannot justify disrupting the rest of the family by spending all day and night in the quest for a bass or two.

Deep water, being a relatively stable habitat, holds not only a greater variety of fish, but also makes them feel less cautious and therefore more likely to grab a bait. Garfish, mullet, mackerel and small pollack usually feed on and off all day, and are predictably active around dawn and dusk. Most species, including the conger eel, also adapt their life-styles to the man-made environment of ports and harbours.

If fishing boats clean their nets in the middle of the day, the chances are that rays, congers and other scavengers will home in on the free food that comes their way. Sometimes, amazingly tolerant of bright sunlight and crystal-clear water, they feed as confidently as their open-coast relatives do only at night.

The message is obvious for anglers intent on sampling the best that Britain can offer. As a trip on its own, or in conjunction with the family vacation, rock and harbour fishing is far too good to miss. You don't need expensive or specialised tackle, baits are no problem, and by playing your cards right you can even divide your fishing time into before breakfast and after supper periods that won't disturb the rest of the family.

Wrasse

Ballan wrasse move close inshore as soon as the water temperatures rise in spring. One of the most predictable angling species, ballans are easy to hook, colourful and robust, though rarely easy to extricate from their rock and weed lairs. On average they weigh 1–3lb; 4lb and over is exceptionally heavy for most waters. Fortunately for them, they are just about the worst possible fish

80

*Fish become used to living in the turmoil of a busy harbour. Mullet feed
around the fishing boats, while rays and pollack hunt among the weeds.*

for the table, resembling oily cotton wool, no matter how well cooked. They
compensate by being tough little fighters, one of the few that feed better
during the day. Rare among fish, the ballan wrasse lies down at night for a
nap.

Wrasse spend a great deal of their time browsing among weeds and rocks
at the water's edge, coming so close inshore that inexperienced fishermen
usually overcast. The trick on most wrasse marks is to begin fishing directly
under the rod tip, and gradually work outwards until the shoal is located.
Float and leger tackle are equally ranked in terms of efficiency and fun, but
legering usually draws the bigger specimens because they live very close to,
or on, the sea-bed. On the other hand, float fishing covers far more ground
and thus gives you a definite edge when the fish are hard to locate or feeding
off the bottom.

Legering in wrasse country means losing tackle, so wise fishermen prefer
disposable sinkers – old nuts and bolts, sparking plugs or stones – and simple

(Above) The ballan wrasse: strictly a fun fish according to the sea fishing experts.

(Right) Light float tackle is excellent for wrasse fishing in fairly clear ground. Otherwise, use a standard beach rod and reel.

(Left) Sheer heaven. A wild rocky cove, full of wrasse, rays and the occasional tope.

one-hook rigs tied without leader or swivels. Although a standard beach rod and reel completely outgun the wrasse itself, they are often essential to deal with the snags. The best bait by far is a small hardback crab. Float fishing is safe enough with a spinning or carp rod, 10lb line and a sliding float carrying about an ounce of lead. Suitable baits include crab, worms and bits of sand-eel. Tactics are very basic: wait for a bite, then strike as hard as you can and, at the same time, lift the fish away from obstructions. Once into clear water, a wrasse soon fights itself to a standstill. Let it get among the rough stuff, though, and you can safely say goodbye to fish and terminal tackle.

Conger Eels

Fishing for big conger from the cliffs is strictly for the specialists. Involving long hours, hazardous climbing and a single-mindedness that the carp expert would envy, it falls well beyond the all-rounder's scope. Smaller conger in the 5–25lb class are another matter.

Big conger, like all old fish, are cunning, timid and scarce. That being so, they are inevitably hard to catch. Those characteristics are not shared by smaller eels, especially if they live in a man-made or heavily frequented environment, one example being the inner basin of a deep water harbour. Such 'tame' fish are sometimes willing to feed in conditions that would send an open-coast eel heading for its burrow among the rocks and weeds.

It is probable that the vast majority of harbours support a conger population, but regional variations in depth, clarity and bait-fish availability ensure that the Atlantic-washed western half of Britain enjoys a distinct advantage. It is difficult to imagine a harbour in the West Country and Wales that does *not* hold enough eels to justify some serious fishing. Sometimes they live happily enough in only a couple of feet of water at low tide; as a rule, however, the greater the depth, the better the sport.

To catch a conger you need a fairly heavy rod, for despite what the light tackle brigade say, a conger of any size is a pretty tough customer who makes full use of her snaggy habitat when she feels the hook. A moment's slackness in the line, and your eel will have wrapped her tail around a convenient stone or rammed her snout into a crack between the jetty pilings. Usually that means checkmate in the eel's favour.

An ordinary beach rod does the trick well enough, but the reel should be a medium multiplier loaded with 25lb line running on to a 50lb shock leader. Slide a sinker on to the end of the leader, tie on a swivel then add a 12-inch trace of 100lb wire or 150lb long-line nylon supporting a 4/0–6/0 Model Perfect or stainless O'Shaughnessy hook. Best baits are fresh mackerel, big sand-eels and frozen squid.

Work your way along the harbour wall or jetty in fifteen-yard stages, fishing the bait along the band of sea-bed lying between the wall or pilings to

A 15lb conger netted from a Jersey shore mark. A landing-net is far better than gaffing for small eels.

about fifty yards out. Longer casts are rarely necessary; the majority of harbour conger are taken within twenty yards of the water's edge. A biting eel might play with a bait for five minutes before making off. Then the rules are the same as those for wrasse fishing. Strike hard and haul the fish away from the snags. The best way to land conger weighing up to about 15lb is by net, not by gaffing. It is not only easier but also reduces injury to the fish (and sometimes to the fisherman). Most fishermen return their eels to the sea.

Mackerel and Garfish

Mackerel and garfish are pelagic fish, which means that they spend most of their lives swimming and feeding in open water rather than near the sea-bed. The garfish, with its eel-shaped body and long snout, could never be confused with the sleek lines of a mackerel, but for angling purposes both species can be considered as one. They often shoal and feed together, prefer similar habitats and are caught by exactly the same tactics. Consequently, mixed bags are commonplace.

85

(Above) Mackerel and garfish attack baits drifted downstream under a float.

(Left) Haddock are a rare treat for northern rock anglers.

(Right) Moonlight on Valencia in Eire, haunt of pollack, conger and rays.

Being essentially plankton feeders, garfish and mackerel are highly dependent on water temperature, sunlight and sea currents. Wherever the clouds of plankton are borne by the ocean, these fish must follow. Their first appearance in British waters is around May, with isolated groups moving into deep water marks around the rocks. As the days lengthen into high summer, plankton blooms and water temperatures rise, the shoals grow bigger, move into the surface layers, and begin feeding in earnest with a noticeable acceleration at dawn and dusk.

As the sun sets and daytime breezes die to leave the sea oily-calm, mackerel make their presence obvious by splashing and swirling in their pursuit of bait-fish. Sometimes huge shoals work their way across the bay, driving their prey literally on to the beach. All it takes to catch fish after fish is a spinner or a bunch of feathers aimed into the killing zone.

During the day, the big shoals generally move into deeper water and are far more likely to be found miles out than within casting range of the beach.

The garfish is known as the 'sea snipe', for obvious reasons.

Smaller groups of mackerel stay inshore, and in particular they concentrate in the tide races created by ebb and flood currents ripping around headlands, harbour mouths and piers. Sometimes they feed right on the surface, but more commonly they hunt in mid-water. The same environment suits garfish to perfection, hence the strong tendency for the two species to compete for the same food – and for the angler's bait.

Mackerel and gars respond well to float fishing and spinning. Sometimes spinning works better when the fish are highly active, but as a rule a piece of fish strip floated downstream accounts for heavier catches in daylight, perhaps because a fish has more time to inspect the bait and is also tempted by the oils and blood oozing from it. Whatever the tactics, a pike or carp rod and fixed-spool reel are the perfect weapons, giving excellent casting range, delicate presentation and enough muscle to control a hooked fish, but without overwhelming it. Both species fight extremely well on the light tackle, and the garfish is renowned for the way it jumps.

Pollack

The inshore pollack has an ecological role similar to that of chub in rivers. Both are predators and opportunists with strong territorial instincts, and both lurk near weed beds and obstructions with the aim of grabbing any small fish which makes the mistake of coming too close. Usually attacking from below, a pollack zooms out of cover, grabs its meal and dives back to its stronghold. The angler's main problem is to stop him making that dive. All other aspects of pollack angling are subordinate to the need to stay in command while the hooked fish attempts to make his headlong rush to safety.

Like most summer species, pollack move in and out of our inshore waters in response to temperature and sunlight intensity. Often quite late to arrive, they should nevertheless be well established along rocky coastlines by June. As a rough but useful rule of thumb, it is worth remembering that the size of pollack parallels the ruggedness of the coastline and the sea's power. To catch big ones upwards of 5lb, it is essential to fish from exposed headlands with

Pollack are fish of rough ground and powerful water.

89

Scraps and guts thrown over the side from trawlers attract congers and rays.

Probably the finest rock marks in Europe: the Blasket Islands in South-west County Kerry.

Pollack and wrasse live just beyond the white water.

Simple but effective baits for summer fishing. Cockles raked from the sand near the low tide mark.

Caution must be the watchword on steep, high cliffs.

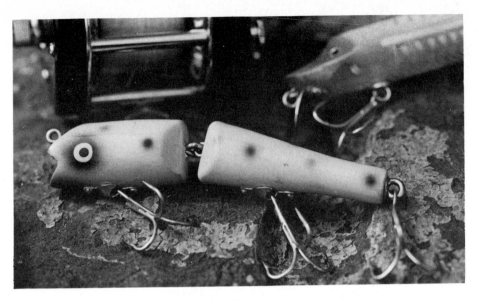

Plug baits are highly effective for inshore predators like bass and pollack.

deep, weedy gullies washed by the swells. Harbour, pier and estuary fish are far more likely to be under 4lb, and the majority will be hardly more than yearling stock. A great attraction for junior anglers, who love catching them one after another, they are a thorough nuisance if you have bigger fish in mind. Sometimes it is impossible to drop a bait through the teeming millions to the quiet depths where the bigger fish lie.

Pollack are catchable on legered or floated baits, but spinning with an artificial or natural lure is the only way to extract the best sport. Pollack hooked on static baits are dull and slow by comparison with a fish of the same weight lured on a spoon or slowly spun eel. Additionally, lure fishing covers considerably more ground. The bigger fish swim in small shoals or singly, so you usually need to work harder to find them and spinning is the perfect tactic for exploring vast areas of sea-bed relatively quickly. Drop a legered bait just fifteen yards short of the right spot and you won't get a single pollack bite all day.

Tackle losses are inevitable on good pollack ground. Artificial lures and complex traces are therefore a waste of money and they catch no more fish than a small dead sand-eel mounted on a long-shank hook, trailed about a yard behind a bullet or barrel sinker. The weight required depends upon water depth and tide strength; on the whole, 1–2oz does the trick. Cast the rig, let it sink on to the bottom or as close as you dare go because of the snags, then retrieve it slowly in sink and draw fashion. There is no mistaking the sudden, vicious attack followed by the crash dive. Unless your reel's clutch is pre-set, a 3lb fish will snap 10lb line as if it were cotton.

93

AUTUMN

6

Coarse Fishing

Autumn is a frustrating time for the all-rounder because there is so much excellent sport from which to choose: bass, whiting and early cod from the beaches and boats, superb reservoir trout and a wealth of coarse fishing. From September to late October it seems as though the underwater world has gone mad. Recovered from spawning and feeding hard in preparation for winter, most species are further boosted by the increase in oxygen level that usually occurs when temperatures go down and freshening winds stir the water's surface. Perhaps it is simply that fish, like anglers, enjoy autumn more than any other season.

Perch are by far the most colourful of British coarse fish.

River Chub

A slug creeps through the bankside vegetation, loses its grip and plops into the water. Almost before it has begun to sink comes a flash of bronze and a swirling splash. The slug disappears into the throat of a hefty chub, which drifts back to its lair under an alder bush to await its next victim. Insect, worm, frog or even a baby vole, they are all on the chub's autumn menu. This preoccupation with food dropping into the water is also many a big chub's downfall.

Of all the baits that chub will accept, slugs come very high on the list. Tough and juicy on the hook, fat slugs are also easy to collect in the early morning before the dew has risen, or in the evening of a rainy day. When the ground is wet they move freely over paths and lawns, but most of the time they hide themselves under vegetation. An hour's work should provide more than enough for a day's chub fishing, and they can be stored for several days in a ventilated plastic container loosely filled with damp newspaper.

Tackle for this style of chub fishing is compact and simple. A strong size 10–4 hook is tied directly to reel line of about 6lb breaking strain. There is usually no need for shot, float or anything else on the line. This freelining system ensures that the bait moves perfectly naturally in the water. Casting is no problem because a slug itself is heavy enough to travel thirty yards or more with ease. Rod design is important, though: a distinctly lazy middle-action blank aids casting accuracy and general tackle control. These are

(Above) A fat, juicy slug for bait. The hook is nicked into the 'saddle'.

(Right) Cast upstream, and drop the slug into every likely looking spot.

(Left) A river chub safely in the landing-net.

characteristics of fibreglass rather than of the latest carbon-fibre materials, hence the preference of some expert chub anglers for Avon-type rods dating back to the early 1970s.

Fishing tactics are based on a roving approach, usually with the angler working his way upstream and exploring all the likely holding areas: eddies, beneath overhangs and bushes, in deep holes and glides. By casting above the fish and letting the current bring the slug back towards him, an angler not only increases his control, but also enhances the quality of presentation. If a stretch of river has not been fished this way for a month or two, chub probably won't be deterred by a slightly second-rate technique, but it is a very different matter when the fish have already been hooked or badly scared. It takes a real expert to winkle out respectably sized chub consistently when the going gets really tough on a hard fished river. On the other hand, some would say that therein lies the real challenge.

A fat chub hooked on slug cast into the eddy where it lives.

(Right) Zander prefer slack, deep water.

Zander

The zander is a foreign invader. Resembling a cross between a pike and a perch, it arrived in Britain from Europe and since establishing itself in the upper East Anglian waterways has spread far afield, into gravel pits and stillwaters. Despite widespread anti-zander sentiments among matchmen and others who watched their favourite species mopped up by this active predator, plenty of fishermen do welcome them. Unquestionably some waters have been stocked deliberately, albeit without the knowledge and approval of either the water authorities or the owners. Does the zander deserve its killer image? Almost certainly not; if stocks are balanced to what the water can support, the benefits probably outweigh the disadvantages. The result can be excellent sport for specialist and all-rounder alike.

There is an easy way to find out where zander live locally: just ask the matchmen! Downstream of the middle reaches of rivers, Fenland drains and stillwaters account for the majority of fish because they offer depth and minimal currents. Within any given water, shoals of zander may be residents or travellers, depending on circumstances. The big question is whether they can be persuaded to feed. Despite their reputation for killing everything in sight, zander can be extremely fussy indeed. Temperature, air pressure, water clarity and light intensity are major factors in the equation.

Zander have a strong liking for semi-darkness. Plenty of depth and colour to the water assist in reducing light penetration, and of course an overcast day is much more to their liking than harsh sunshine. By the same token, dawn and dusk usually prompt an urge to feed. Temperature and air pressure go hand in hand during late autumn and winter, due to the meteorological link between them. Warmer than normal periods – perhaps better described as ice and frost-free – are always associated with Atlantic depressions. Depressions also bring heavy cloud and rain, which add to their attraction. So critical are these factors that in their absence some zander experts would not bother to go fishing from the tail-end of autumn onwards. For most of the season, however, cloud cover and a ripple on the water are sufficient to switch on the zander, especially towards dusk. Hook one zander, and almost certainly you'll have discovered a pack of fish, for they are quite gregarious compared with most predators. Even the big fellows hunt in small groups.

Tackle and tactics are scaled-down versions of what you might use for pike. A 10lb line and a medium-action rod of about 1½lb test curve will handle a big zander yet allow small ones to show their mettle. Far from an outstanding fighter, a zander is completely outgunned by tackle any heavier. A small live or dead fish presented on a leger or paternoster completes the outfit. The normal trace is designed on pike lines but with smaller hooks. If there are no pike around, a Dacron trace is tough enough to withstand the fish's jaws. Otherwise, use wire just in case. Tactics also follow the pike theme: work along the bank, dropping baits into likely looking spots until the group of

Two hefty Suffolk zander for specimen hunter Barry Waldron.

Zander country – overcast skies and falling pressure, with the water ruffled by a mild south-westerly wind.

fish is located. Sometimes a fish picks up the bait and runs immediately, but mostly the attack is quite shy and prolonged before anything positive happens. Patience is the key word.

Perch

Perch are set to become the success story of the 1980s. Ravaged by disease to the point of disappearance on some waters, they have begun to return with a vengeance. Stillwaters, canals and some rivers now carry a head of sizeable fish running beyond the 3lb mark, which for many anglers is the perch of a lifetime. Their appearance in trout reservoirs is an interesting development, perhaps pointing the way to where the really big specimens will be concentrated. Like pike, they seem to thrive exceedingly well in such surroundings, although quite why they do is unclear. The 'obvious' suggestion that they eat small trout is probably either untrue or of minor consequence. It is more likely that their growth rate has much to do with being left alone to grow fat on small roach and other coarse species which many a trout fishery supports in huge and unmolested numbers.

While perch are still in the process of re-establishing themselves, angling prospects need to be judged in the right perspective. As a consistently successful project for the all-rounder, they come low on the list. Most waters do not

(Left) Perch hunt along the margins of the weed beds and reeds.

(Right) A polystyrene ball suspends the live bait at the correct fishing depth.

(Below, left) Perch are highly predatory, so live baits are always excellent for the bigger ones.

(Below, right) A bag of perch that would have been impossible to catch when the species was affected by disease.

hold enough to justify the time and effort, and for the foreseeable future that trend will continue. However, new specimen perch strongholds are developing all the time and in the most unlikely places, so it is inevitable that before long one of your local fishing spots will suddenly switch itself on. *Suddenly* is the operative word; overnight the water starts producing fish. In fact, the usual explanation is that noboby has deliberately set out to fish for them until then. The fish must have been around for years; how else would they have grown so big? Only when somebody catches one by accident does the word get out – and then of course every perch enthusiast for miles around heads for the same swim.

Small perch are not worth catching. More significantly, they are a thorough nuisance. Their enthusiasm for pouncing on small baits immediately they hit the water is a godsend for small boys, perhaps, but effectively rules out serious fishing for bigger perch, or, indeed, coarse species of many kinds that eat worms or maggots. Ways to discriminate between the babies and the specimens are by spinning and live baiting with a small roach or rudd – or even a two to three-inch perch.

Spinning is a hit-or-miss affair in most waters, and no guarantee of sifting out the best fish. Even so, it should not be dismissed out of hand. Small spoons, plugs and spinners all catch fish that are feeding actively in open water, and there is no denying that when the plan comes together properly, catching perch this way is more exciting and productive than any other technique.

Probably 75 per cent of perch over 2lb caught by intent (rather than by accident, as most big fish actually are) fall to a small live bait cast alongside the reeded margins, edges of weed beds, or into the deep holes where perch love to hunt. Their coloration and stripes offer a clue to their tactics of lying in wait until a small fish comes within grabbing range.

For that reason, it usually pays to cover as much water as possible rather than leave the bait in one spot for hours on end. Besides, when perch are feeding hard they often attack within seconds of the bait dropping into the water. The longer you have to wait, the longer the odds become of a perch homing in. Although far from an infallible rule, it does underline the sense in keeping tackle on the move, especially at dawn and dusk when the fish are noticeably more active than in the middle of the day. A simple float rig with a single hook through the bait's lip and just enough shot to maintain fishing depth does the trick. An Avon-type rod, 6lb line and fixed spool completes the outfit.

Eels

Small eels are pretty disgusting creatures to catch. Big eels are such a different proposition that it would be far better for their reputation if anglers thought

Unlike small, slimy 'bootlace' eels, big ones are a worthwhile challenge.

Eels lie quietly if turned on to their backs. They must not be left too long in that position, however.

of them as being an entirely separate species. In the richness of autumn coarse fishing, good eels are an opportunity never to be missed. It must be pointed out that the all-rounder's chances of hitting into a big fish in the 5lb-plus bracket vary from slim to moderate. No matter, it just has to be worth making the effort if one of your local stillwaters is known for its eels. For the sake of convenience, the ideal plan is to combine a night session with a spot of carp or late season tenching.

Eels eat all manner of meaty food, but as far as hook baits go, a chunk of dead fish or a small dead bait takes some beating. Tactics are very simple indeed: cast the bait into a swim known to produce big eels and wait for something to turn up. On most nights nothing happens, which is no great loss if you are catching fish on the other rods. Now and again along will come a hefty eel that sneaks away with your bait. Give it time to move off, then whack the hook in. During the next five or ten minutes you'll discover why they are so highly prized for their dogged, powerful fighting. Round two begins when they reach land!

7

Saltwater Opportunities

Whether you prefer sea, lake or river, autumn offers a huge range of opportunities. Asked to choose their favourite season, the majority of experienced fishermen would elect that magic spell from September to mid-November. It is the pinnacle of nature's achievement, a time when all the threads are drawn together: healthy fish, large stocks, perfect water and kind weather. The fisherman's only problem is to pack everything in before the onset of winter.

In the marine world, autumn's influence is as evident in the waves and currents as in the fish population. Owing to the relative position of the earth, moon and sun during the autumn equinox, September and October spring tides are among the biggest of the year and are often associated with changeable weather. October gales are a notorious feature of the natural pattern, sometimes blasting the coastline so hard that fishing is impossible for days on end. Even if the winds are more gentle, the tidal and weather cycles trigger a lowering of water temperatures which, in turn, prompt the summer species to move out while encouraging the winter stocks to come closer. This is good news for the fisherman, who can expect mixed bags of whiting, bass, rays and flat-fish. Sometimes the front runners of the cod will arrive before the bass depart south. In all, you can expect the unexpected.

Beach Fishing

Autumn fishing in the West of Britain is basically an extension of the summer; more intense and slightly easier, perhaps, but comprised of essentially the same species and tactics. In the East and South-east it is another matter. Summer beach sport in these regions is rather limited, with little but eels and flatties on offer unless you are lucky enough to drop a bait in front of a big bass or a smoothhound. Whiting change all that. Invading the inshore waters in vast numbers, these pearlescent, perky little hunters transform the angling scene and the fisherman's fortunes. Where a beach was devoid of anglers in August, it will be crammed to capacity from late September onwards. By the end of October, it might be impossible to find space to cast.

That whiting are amazingly simple to hook, totally lacking in fight and among the messiest of fish to handle matters not one bit to the hundreds of thousands of enthusiastic anglers whose entire calendar begins and ends with the arrival and departure of the autumn invasion. Heap what scorn you like

(Above) The whiting's big eyes and lack of barbule are key points in telling it apart from a small codling.

(Left) Whiting are easy to catch by the dozen, even if you have never been to the beach before.

(Right) A two hook paternoster is the right basis for autumn, when the fish are small and of mixed types.

on its sporting merit, but you will never dent the whiting's image. Even cod and bass experts who sniff disdainfully at the mention of whiting still sneak off for a few frantic, slimy sessions. After a while, whiting bashing does become a boring treadmill of baiting, casting and cranking in another two or three suicidal little fish. To begin with, however, it makes a pleasant contrast to the hard, unproductive summer just past.

Whiting fishing is not simply a matter of tactics, tackle and baits. Its real attraction is the atmosphere generated by warm sunsets, calm water, and the hiss and glow of paraffin lamps bursting into life as night falls. There is no better introduction to beach angling, so it is no coincidence that most dedicated beach anglers along the east and south coasts began their apprenticeship when the equinox tides brought the whiting within casting range.

Early in the season, before the shoals become well distributed along the coast, the lion's share of sport comes from isolated beaches which are perennially attractive for some reason. Among the key factors is depth: a steeply shelving beach with plenty of cover at low water normally produces three to five times more fish, most of which are caught after dark. Indeed, the difference between day and night fishing is as clear-cut as if somebody had flicked a switch. By day, your tackle lies untouched; within an hour of darkness falling, whiting rip baits to shreds as soon as they land in the water.

The popularity of autumn beach fishing sometimes poses serious threats to foreshore ecology if the worm beds are over-dug.

Any rod and reel capable of delivering a 4–5oz paternoster rig more than fifty yards will catch whiting perfectly well, but any limitations in their design will become apparent when cod arrive later in the year. Because most new-comers who begin with whiting eventually progress into general shore fishing, there is a lot to be said for kitting yourself out with a proper beach casting outfit from the start.

A fast action rod, 11½–12-foot long, balanced to cast about 5oz of lead (most of today's better rods are actually matched to 150g) ensures the correct blend of casting power, bite sensitivity and precise handling. Even a cheap rod built to those specifications will cast a bait well beyond the 125-yard mark, which, though far from essential for whiting, is no more than par for the course with cod. The reel can be a casting multiplier or a fixed spool; the choice is a matter of personal preference. A 12–15lb main line is ideal, and is protected from snapping during the cast by the insertion of a 40–50lb leader between it and the terminal rig. The most popular rig is a two or three hooked paternoster with short snoods and fine wire Aberdeen hooks. Baited with pieces of absolutely fresh mackerel or herring and tipped with worms if necessary, this simplest of traces is deadly for whiting and very easy to tie and cast.

Bonus Species

Knowledgeable fishermen accept that there are two distinct bass populations: school fish running up to the 8lb mark, and much heavier fish which hunt alone or in small groups. As a rule, school fish are far more sensitive to the changes in water temperature and habitat that take place in the North Sea and Channel from September onwards. The farther west you go, the longer they stay inshore because of the Atlantic Ocean's warming influence.

Big bass also respond to the approach of autumn, but their habits are virtually opposite to those of the smaller fish. Around 75 per cent of the annual crop of specimen bass topping the 10lb mark, and closer to 90 per cent of the monsters over 13lb, are caught long after the whiting have arrived. Most are hooked at extremely short range from beaches where small bass are uncommon even at peak season. Why this is, nobody really understands. What we do know is that Felixstowe, Aldeburgh, the Crouch estuary, Dungeness and Chesil Beach, among others, can be relied upon to produce a small but highly significant annual crop of what could be termed 'freaks'. A handful of exceptionally dedicated beach fishermen catch such fish by design. Otherwise, it is purely a matter of luck. There is always an element of fortune in angling, however, so it could be that swimming among this season's whiting is a massive fish with your name on it.

The sole is another species that often remains close inshore during autumn. Highly prized for the table, it is as hard a fighter, pound for pound, as any

The most prized flat-fish of them all, the sole. Big fish turn up along the east and south coasts in late autumn.

School bass begin to move south when autumn winds cool the water.

(Left) Dabs live on clean sand, and are classed among the tastiest fish in the sea. They are common in autumn.

fish. It also enjoys a unique position in that most very big sole are hooked from the beach rather than a boat. In fact, it might be quite easy to break the boat sole record by anchoring a dinghy about fifty yards offshore and casting into the back of the surfline.

Smaller than the sole, but in some people's opinion a far tastier fish, is the dab. Similar in appearance to a flounder, but rough to the touch when brushed along the back from tail to head, this lively little flat-fish becomes ever more active as autumn progresses. Like bass and sole, it usually turns up during a whiting session, and, because it responds to precisely the same tackle, tactics and baits, requires no special attention at this time of year.

Until October, whiting are not particularly enthusiastic about living in estuaries. There, the emphasis remains on the two species that provided fair sport during the summer: flounders and eels. Eels are a fish that some anglers love and others hate. Personally, I like catching them. Despite horror stories about their ability to tie traces in knots and cover everything with slime, they are quite a challenge. Small eels are suicidal pests, but bigger fish topping the 2lb mark can be exceedingly difficult to lure. Again, ordinary beach paternoster tackle does the trick. Most baits catch a few fish, but peeler crab is the supreme killer.

Silver eels topping the 2lb mark are a sporting proposition, and exceptionally good to eat.

Monster bass in the 13–17lb class turn up all around the southern coastline, most being caught by accident.

Inshore Boat Casting

A boat casting trip should be on every all-round angler's agenda at this time of year. Whiting are a boring prospect unless you enjoy catching literally hundreds of fish, two, three or even four at once depending on the length of the paternoster. The rays have long gone, and what tope remain are in pretty poor condition compared to what they were in late spring. There are, however, two species that more than compensate: sandbank bass and shallow water smoothhounds.

Sandbank fishing is identical to surf casting, except that you cast from a boat. Throughout the main run of ebb and flood tides, water forces its way across the gullies and sandbanks with such power that on the stillest of days the sea erupts into rolling lines of surf along the sandbank edges. Running up from perhaps thirty feet to six feet in less than fifty yards, the current rips marine creatures from their burrows, disorientates the free-swimmers such as whitebait and sand-eels, and oxygenates the water. It is the perfect habitat for bass, which of all species are at their happiest in surging, foaming breakers.

Finding the fish is the skipper's job; yours is to trundle a chunk of king ragworm or a live sand-eel through the rough stuff. Cast on a simple one-hook leger, the bait is swept up the face of the bank – and into the fish's

117

For fun and fight, nothing beats a smoothhound hooked in shallow water.

Big bass: one reason why anglers throughout Britain travel to the east coast ports each autumn.

A bass caught on king ragworm drifted in the rough water visible in the background.

mouth. Such a simple technique somehow fails to square with the generally accepted view that bass are difficult to catch, but for a few glorious autumn weeks when tides are right, it really is a piece of cake.

According to discerning fishermen, the smoothhound is the only dogfish worth catching. Actually it is not a true dogfish. The relationship is close, and rather obvious when you see the fish whose body is powerful and fairly streamlined, with a subtle hint of tope. Teeth are arranged in flat pavements like those of a ray. Grey on the back and flanks, white below, a smoothhound is plain by comparison to the bull huss. There are two common species caught by anglers: the starry smoothhound, so called because of its stellate white spots, and the common. (Just to confuse matters, however, some commons are spotted, and some starries are plain. Dental examination is the real key to identification.)

Light tackle, rolling lead and ragworm or sand-eel bait are the right formula for inshore bassing.

Small school bass will snatch lures without a moment's hesitation.

Smoothhounds like fast water and undulating ground, but are never keen on surf. Instead, they roam much closer to shore, along the edges of the mud-flats and channels in estuary mouths. The Solent, Blackwater and Thames estuaries are classic marks for those very reasons. The packs of fish are continually on the move, seldom staying put for more than a few days at a time. Success is almost entirely dependent on your skipper's experience and day to day familiarity with the fishing grounds. As with the bass, tackle and tactics are very simple. Use boat casting tackle armed with a single hook rig, and cast exactly where the skipper tells you. Hermit crabs are the most successful bait by far, and are caught in a drop net hung over the side of the boat. All you really need to concentrate on is the one golden rule of smooth-hound fishing: always pre-set the reel's drag, and never try to stop a hooked fish in its tracks. An average smoothhound of 10–15lb will snap 30lb line with absolute ease should you try to hold back its first run.

WINTER

8

River Fishing

Flushed by late autumn rains and frost, a river and its banks spend winter in relative hibernation. This is not so for many of the fish, however. Congregating in eddies, backwaters and deep holes, they feed steadily provided that temperatures stay high enough to provoke activity and hunger. In addition, the tendency to shoal is higher during winter and in the run-up to spring spawning. Pike are an excellent example. From February onwards, they invade shallow dykes and tributaries where they not only feed well but exhibit a lack of caution never seen at other times.

With the emphasis on good sport, more precise swim location and sometimes easier fishing, the river in winter is always an excellent prospect for the all-rounder. When stillwaters are frozen solid and saltwater action slows in classic style during the early New Year, rivers with enough flow to keep the ice at bay offer the last hope of wetting a line.

Types of river and target species are interlinked. On the whole, a slow river offers much better bream fishing than chubbing, for example, simply because the former prefers sluggish water, while the latter shows a strong inclination to live and feed in a faster-moving environment. Although there are always exceptions, in the quest for good fishing with minimum preparation and economy of effort, these general rules must always be considered.

Chub

Chub are the equivalent of saltwater pollack, sharing many of their characteristics and habits. Powerful, fairly streamlined fish with a strong liking for heavy cover on the edge of swirling currents, they feed essentially by ambushing small animals and fish, but are far from averse to scavenging. Being masters of their ecological slot, they are not used to being pushed around, which in turn makes them quite easy to deceive when they are in feeding mood, and also provokes a powerful fight. This is not to say that chub fishing is absolutely simple, requiring nothing in the way of skill. Like all fish, they can be frustratingly devious and uncooperative, but their nature and life-style ensure that on occasion they will fall for almost any bait drifted their way. Natural, artificial, static or on the move, any kind of bait is potentially successful, depending on season and the chub's mood.

In winter the emphasis must be on static or slow-moving natural baits.

Extracting a chub from its lair among the tree roots.

Cold water makes all fish sluggish, so they appreciate time to creep up and inspect their food. Attractive scents may induce a take when movement and vibration fail to convince the fish that here is something too good to miss. In contrast, competition for food is inevitably higher when fish are working in shoals. In those circumstances, a float-fished bait may catch a fish's eye before something lying on the bottom would, causing him to attack before the other fish move in.

Many clean, reasonably fast-moving rivers still support a fair head of chub. Most at risk among those that fit the correct general description are rivers which have had their banks 'improved' by landowners and the water authorities. Denuded of weed beds, overhanging bushes and trees, deep holes and underwater roots, a river is immediately less attractive to chub. They move elsewhere and ultimately become scarce or absent. It is an ever more common scenario which affects a river's long-term stability and prospects in general.

Chub Tactics

Two approaches pay off with winter chub: moving from one likely hot spot to the next, taking one or two fish from each, or building up a single heavy

(Above) Like peas in a pod: 2lb chub taken on trotted bread.

(Left) Shoals of small chub in open water are located and caught by trotting.

A fast-flowing chub swim on the Norfolk Wensum.

bag by concentrating on an open-water swim where fish are known to shoal in reasonable numbers. In the latter case, tactics are based on steady feeding with mashed bread or equally substantial ground bait, while trotting a hook bait through the swim or trundling it along the bottom. Sport can be fast and furious as fish compete for passing food, and may continue long enough for the angler to amass 50lb of fish in the 1–3lb class. Bigger fish do swim among the shoal, but in general they prefer to be solitary.

Sitting it out all day in one spot does not appeal to many anglers, especially in the depths of winter. A roving approach not only keeps you reasonably

127

A chunk of crust topped by bread paste for extra security on the hook.

warm, but covers far more water and, again as a general rule, produces bigger fish. Tactics are basically the same as before but on a smaller scale. A few handfuls of soaked bread, or a slice or two drifted along the surface, are introduced under overhangs and into deep holes and eddies, followed by a freelined, floated or lightly legered hook bait. A static bait presented on the bottom has considerable appeal because a chub has more time to locate it and attack. Torpid from the cold water, it may not notice or be quick enough to react to a bait passing by.

Roach

All fish react to bright lights, mostly adversely. Roach are so remarkably sensitive that sport turns on and off in step with illumination levels. On dull days, especially when the river is running coloured after a flood, they may feed from dawn to dusk. In sunlit, clear water they refuse all offerings until dusk falls. The decision to go roach fishing should therefore take these factors into account. If conditions are wrong, think seriously about another species or venue. Similarly, very cold conditions reduce the likelihood of making a catch. The perfect scenario for excellent roach fishing can be summed up as a warm, dull day or evening with the river moving well and having lost the gin-clearness typical of late autumn.

Roach shoal throughout winter where the river swirls around the deep bend.

Roach Tactics

Trotting and legering are the main ways to catch winter roach. Trotting is a lovely way to catch fish that depends on your swim being long and fairly evenly running to permit the necessary tackle and baiting control. Bread flake and maggots are both excellent baits, presented on line of around 2½lb breaking strain, with the lighter hook length if fish are especially shy. A 12 or 13-foot match rod and closed-face reel completes the outfit, although the purists would insist on a centre pin reel instead.

Where currents and depths do not allow successful trotting, light legering against a quivertip indicator, or laying on with a float set slightly over depth, and a BB or near equivalent shot resting on the bottom, are much more practical. Being static once in position, but still manoeuvrable enough to be presented with great accuracy in holes, runs and eddies, the bait is much more likely to be found and picked up. Ground and hook baits are similar to those used in trotting, perhaps with more emphasis on not overfeeding and disturbing the fish. On a similar theme, some roach anglers prefer a swimfeeder set-up so that their ground bait is controlled far more precisely than it could ever be by hand.

A fat roach in the peak of winter condition.

(Above) Norwich tackle dealer John Wilson casts into a typical winter roach swim – slow water with plenty of colour and depth.

(Right) Sunset until dusk is a highly productive period on the winter river.

Bream

As a fish for the all-rounder, the bream has strong points for and against it. The hours or days spent surveying a water to locate the shoals – dead time if you could be fishing for another species – are balanced against the chances of ending the day with a total weight almost impossible to achieve with any other river or stillwater species.

Bream live in the lower, siltier-bottomed areas of slow-running rivers where, in a similar manner to a herd of grazing cows, they root through the mud to find their food. Highly attracted to properly compounded ground baits, they are a straightforward proposition in terms of tackle and techniques. It is in the pattern of their movements along a stretch of river that bream create so much confusion. Here one day, gone the next, they are even harder to pin-point in winter because the characteristic bubbles produced by feeding shoals are nowhere near as pronounced and easily spotted as they are in summer, when the fish may even roll and wallow as they move from one feeding place to the next.

On the other hand, bream tend to congregate on a semi-permanent basis during winter and can thus be narrowed down to within about a half-mile stretch. Exactly where they are and whether they feed is determined by

Filling a swimfeeder with maggots.

Mixing wheat with mashed bream to make ground bait for bream.

132

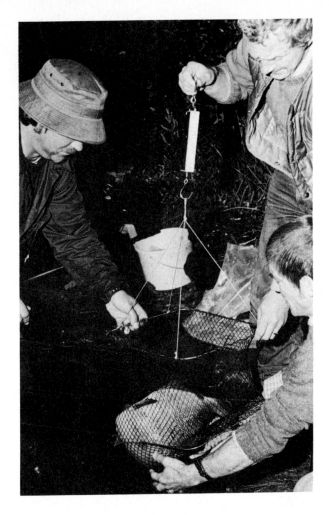

Most big bream are caught at night. This 10lb specimen came just before midnight.

conditions – they like warm, overcast weather and some colour in the water – and by angling pressures. Big matches result in so much feed carpeting the river bottom that every fish in the shoal is stuffed to the gills. There is some evidence that over-baiting also sours the bottom and deters further feeding. If you happen to cast in the right spot, good sport is there for the taking. Otherwise it is a matter of either hopping from one likely place to the next or staying put until a shoal moves into the area. Both tactics have their devotees.

The only way to improve your success rate is by living on top of the water and checking on the shoals' movements day by day. Otherwise, bream fishing for the all-rounder is inevitably a hit-or-miss matter. On balance, however, most keen fishermen consider that visiting the river when good prospects and weather coincide is well worth the effort. After all, a bag topping the hundred-weight mark, with individual fish going up to 5–7lb or bigger, is never to be sneezed at.

133

Three river bream over the 4lb mark, part of a heavy bag on a match-fished water.

Telescopic lips give a clue to the bream's feeding habits.

A particularly pale bream from the lower Suffolk Stour.

9

Pike Fishing

In every branch of angling, one or two species of fish dominate the scene at any given time of year. Although they are far from universally popular, pike rank highest on the list of winter big-fish catches. They are strong fighters, fairly easy to locate and lure, and also the heaviest fish that a coarse angler is ever likely to encounter, other than carp.

It is fortunate that the bad old days of pike fishing have gone. Within living memory, the pike was regarded as a fierce, ravenous killer unworthy of the consideration automatically given to other coarse fish. Most pike hooked in popular match and pleasure fishing waters were killed, without a moment's thought about their ecological role. As a result, waters became choked with immature fish.

A certain anti-pike tendency still exists, particularly in reservoirs and lakes stocked with trout. There is some justification for not liking pike if you happen to prefer fishing for roach, bream and the other species that they eat. Most instances of cruelty and indiscriminate culling occur because the anglers involved understand nothing of the pike's life-style and purpose, and because they are scared stiff by those wicked-looking eyes and jaws. In reality, pike are easy to handle and unhook if you know the right techniques.

Pike Waters

Virtually all waterways from ditches upwards hold pike. Given the right balance between numbers of pike and stocks of bait-fish, the species will survive happily enough in ponds, streams and rivers that do not rate a second glance from keen fishermen. Anyone content to catch small fish will therefore find plenty of opportunities available close to home.

Serious anglers are aware that catching worthwhile pike on a regular basis demands care and effort. Big fish – over 20lb by most pike men's standards – are always a challenge. All points considered, it is probably easier to catch a 20lb carp than a pike of the same weight, one reason being that pike are a truly wild fish, whereas carp have become more and more a farmed species due to the explosion of interest in stocking programmes and baiting techniques.

Successful piking depends upon two factors in particular: the water must be capable of sustaining big fish; and the fish population must itself be balanced to allow a fair proportion of the pike to grow to a decent size.

*(Above) Pike live in the
most unlikely spots. The
common error is to overcast.*

*(Left) A 12-foot medium
action rod of 2–3lb test
curve will handle big pike
with ease, but without
outgunning the smaller
ones.*

Ecological dynamics are extremely complex and are not well understood, even by pike enthusiasts. Like most fishermen, they tend to base many of their 'facts' on tradition, hypothesis and sheer guesswork.

In general, the higher the fish population, the lower their average weight will be. This is by no means an absolute rule, but with pike in particular, the trend is well established, one reason being that only large waters contain a regular supply of the kind of food that makes a pike put on weight in the first place. Pike do not become large by eating massive numbers of small fish. Like all big predators, they eat few, but large, meals. This explains the association between pike and bream or trout. Pike in waters such as the Norfolk Broads grow heavy on bream; elsewhere, excellent piking often goes hand in glove with trout reservoirs – much to the anguish of fly fishermen and owners. Trout-fed pike pick up weight at a tremendous rate, sometimes so quickly that their bodies outstrip their heads. Many big pike taken from food-rich stillwaters are almost grotesque due to their tiny heads and swollen bellies.

Also on a general theme, stillwater pike are heavier than those in rivers and streams. Food supply and population levels are involved, and there is the third factor of water movement. A fish that expends a fair proportion of its energy fighting the current has a lower food conversion rate and therefore grows

Reservoir pumping stations are highly attractive to pike, presumably because they feed on small fish living around the filter pipes. A big pike comes to the net through the dawn fog.

(Right) Small pike may not appeal to the experts, but they ensure plenty of fun and action for the all-rounder.

more slowly. Only rich waters like the Thames, Hampshire Avon, Severn and lowland Irish rivers succeed in challenging stillwater growth rates.

Locating Pike

The quest for big pike is fast becoming a circus. As soon as large fish are located and the news leaks out, a hard core of fanatics and experts descend on the water in question and hammer it day after day. The water suffers, as do the pike themselves and the local anglers who can no longer get a look in. Enthusiasm is all very well, but always carries the risk of giving the sport a bad name. As a consequence, today's pike angler is under increasing pressure to keep quiet. Finding a new water, studying it and catching good fish calls for dedication and no little expense. No wonder that having done all that, many people prefer to stay silent. The news always gets out in the end, though, so it is simply a matter of time until that water is added to the hit list.

For the all-rounder looking for good sport, but realistic enough to know the hazards involved in the pursuit of exceptionally large fish, rivers and gravel pits probably offer the most satisfying balance of effort against results. For every water that holds fish above 20lb, there are dozens which provide superb sport with fish up to the 10–15lb mark. Even in these days of 44lb-plus pike, a 10–12lb fish is still a worthy target. Even an 8lb fish hooked on light tackle from a small river or pond gives great pleasure. There is far more to successful angling than heavyweight catches alone.

A river pike caught from slack water within one rod length of the bank.

A float paternoster rig and electronic buzzer make a useful combination for winter piking.

Pike Techniques

The use of live baits is a key issue in modern piking. The technical side can be argued either way, but the moral question must remain a matter of personal commitment unless legislation decides. Live baiting has been outlawed in some areas, but on the whole it remains an acceptable technique.

Live baits almost certainly catch fish more rapidly than other techniques, and as such are probably to be recommended to the fisherman who enjoys the occasional day's piking. All points considered, a live fish rather than a dead bait or lure increases the chances of success of some kind, often by a considerable margin. Dead baits may well produce as many fish in the long term, and certainly appear to account for a healthy majority of the bigger fish, but these statistics take little account of the time involved. Most fishermen who are not pike specialists are simply not prepared to sit all day – never mind all season – waiting for one run on a dead bait if they could pick up half a dozen nice but smaller fish on live baits.

The results of spinners and other artificial baits are rather more difficult to quantify. Across the board, they probably rank somewhere between live and dead baits. The exception is when pike are particularly active and feeding hard. In those conditions, artificials outfish other techniques with ease. On the other hand, it is said that more pike would be caught on lures if only fishermen would make the effort. In the USA, for example, lures and spinners outclass all other baits and tactics.

Catching pike on artificial lures is not only a viable proposition, but crammed with excitement too.

The catch of a lifetime for many dedicated pike anglers, but quite a routine business for Norfolk's John Watson. All three are over 20lb.

Live Baiting

Many kinds of small fish make successful live baits, but roach and rudd are probably the most popular because they are relatively easy to obtain. Some fishermen swear by more exotic species such as crucian carp, trout, or even goldfish. Whatever the bait, there are two basic live baiting techniques: static fishing involving a paternoster rig of some sort, and drifting. They are used according to whether you intend to tether a bait in a known hot spot, or must search large areas of unknown water.

The float paternoster is versatile, simple to construct and easy to control. Fishing depth is set at the bottom by adjusting the length of nylon between sinker and trace, and at the top by adjusting a stop knot on the reel line which traps the sliding float. The fish is mounted on a pair of barbless double or treble hooks attached to multistrand wire of 15–20lb breaking strain. The rig is then cast gently into a likely looking spot. Sometimes a run occurs almost immediately, sometimes you must wait a long time for the pike to investigate and attack. If nothing happens after half an hour, most anglers would advise checking the bait and recasting it into another potential lie.

Drift techniques use a similar trace system with the lead weights mounted above to prevent the bait from swimming upwards. The float may be either a simple polystyrene ball or fitted with vanes to pick up the wind. In a river, currents move the tackle and the float therefore does nothing more than support the bait and indicate bites. In stillwaters, motive power comes from the wind, so vanes or a miniature sail are essential. It is also important that the line floats on the surface, which is achieved by applying dressing at regular intervals.

Dead Baiting

Dead baits can be fished on the bottom on a leaded trace or freelined, under a float or in semi-floating form controlled by air injection. All methods work, and one of the skills of dead baiting is to discover which approach pays off on the water concerned. Choice of bait is probably more critical than with live baiting, presumably because pike are attracted to dead baits by their appearance and smell. Unless they are fished sink-and-draw, wobbled or are otherwise moving, the pike receives no other powerful stimulus and therefore the strength and attractiveness of the bait's natural scents and oils become the dominant factor. Dead coarse fish lure pike well enough, but mackerel, herring, sprats and smelt usually have the edge because their scent trails are both stronger and longer lasting. Experiments suggest that there is some advantage in the use of colourings and flavourings, but they are by no means universally accepted by the pike fishing fraternity.

Pike can be landed by inserting a finger into the 'chin'.

(Left) Predator and prey.

145

Lure Fishing

Actively hunting pike are attuned to the movement and vibration of their prey. A spinner or plug drawn through the water triggers a decisive attack because the pike is momentarily deceived. The principle is simple enough, and works that way in practice, provided the fish are in feeding mood and willing to chase their prey. This they are more likely to do when the water is

A home-made wooden plug bait responsible for hundreds of pike.

The proper way to support a pike's head – safe for angler and fish alike.

(Left) Pike should be netted, never gaffed.

Sleek and in peak condition, this river pike would be a welcome catch for any pleasure fisherman.

reasonably warm; the metabolic rate of most fish is dictated by their environment, so they do not move as quickly, nor chase so willingly in cold weather. As a result, most lure fishing takes place during summer and early autumn, and is particularly exciting and productive when the fish are hunting around shallow, weeded areas.

In the depths of winter, pike become torpid and their mode of feeding is centred on ambush. Inevitably, they are less inclined to grab a lure unless it passes within easy reach. Even then, the effort sometimes proves too much. In such circumstances live or dead baits are far superior. Yet even in the depths of winter there is sometimes enough sun and warming wind to lift the water temperature sufficiently to make pike far more active, and in those circumstances spinners and plugs are excellent, especially if you can tease the fish into action by drawing the bait past its nose several times.

10

Cod Fishing

Without cod, sea fishing in Britain would sink into obscurity. The waters around these islands offer a standard of winter sport which alone could support the entire tackle and bait industries. Some fishermen are so convinced that cod are the only species worth catching that their tackle lies unused between April and mid-October while the fish are away in offshore northern waters. To the uninitiated this may seem to be an extreme attitude, but for those who have experienced the powerful, dogged fight of a 15lb fish hooked in the surging backwash of a December beach, it is a viewpoint that invokes a great deal of sympathy. Compared to any other species regularly taken from the eastern surf, cod are in a class of their own.

Atrocious conditions, but with cod feeding hard behind the backwash.

Specimen cod can be caught in broad daylight, but the huge majority are night fish exclusively.

Cod like a foreshore broken up with weeds and rocks. The idea that they must have deep water is completely mistaken.

Cod Fisheries

Other than the rock cod that live permanently close inshore in the North of Britain, cod are migratory. The cycle is complex and variable, depending on water temperatures, winds and commercial fishing as well as on the natural ups and downs of breeding efficiency. A few years of heavy, successful spawning put plenty of fish within casting range, more or less regardless of how many the trawlers take from the migrating hordes; bad years inevitably lead to massively reduced stocks in every area. Beach fishing is hit hardest because it is the final link in the chain of events, and highly sensitive to the ill effects of weather and season.

151

The north-east Atlantic cod is a cold water fish with the bulk of stocks concentrated in the upper reaches of the North Sea, such as the Dogger Bank. Owing to the flow of winter currents and winds from the North Polar region, the majority of shoals are funnelled towards East and South-east Britain. There is no shortage on the Atlantic side, but the sport tends to be patchy both in distribution and from season to season. Cod sometimes run into the Clyde or along the Welsh beaches in numbers and size that make the eastern angler jealous. Usually, this western bias occurs during a lean spell in the cod's natural cycle, which spans approximately ten years between troughs. Considered over the full cycle, however, the North Sea and Channel areas account for at least 75 per cent of the rod and line catches. Famous cod beaches like Dungeness, Chesil, Aldeburgh, Orford, Spurne Point and the Yorkshire rock platforms reign supreme. On a good year, the cod invasion guarantees super fishing from virtually any beach touched by those northern currents and winds.

Weather and Time

The first of the winter cod swim into casting range during the latter part of the whiting season, and as their numbers swell, those of the whiting diminish. The two species do not get along together, mainly because the cod eat their smaller cousins. By the middle of November, codding begins in earnest, and, except for a break over Christmas and New Year when the fish become preoccupied with feeding on herrings and sprats, continues until late March at least.

Depending on where you fish, sport may be fairly consistent throughout the period. On most beaches, however, there is a distinct pre-Christmas peak followed by another some time around late February. On both occasions, expect a substantial improvement in the average size of the fish you catch. By contrast, spectacular numbers of tiny fish move inshore just after Christmas, in the aftermath of a heavy spawning season. Seldom above nine inches long, these small codling are a complete pest, stripping the hook so quickly that better fish which may be around stand absolutely no chance of finding your bait. Although a thoroughly exasperating situation, it at least points towards good sport in two or three years.

The exact time to go codding varies so much that it is impossible to single out many factors that really do determine your success rate. Most of the traditional theories are little more than wishful thinking, or perhaps pure coincidence. There is no general rule about tides, for example. Some beaches fish better on the ebb, some on the flood; some come alive nearer the low water stage, others at the opposite end of the cycle. The onus is on the fisherman to discover the pattern of his preferred beaches. Despite all the mumbo-jumbo, however, two factors should always be considered: water

Cod and whiting.

Small codling are the perfect introduction to sea angling.

movement and light intensity.

The movement of the tide switches the cod's appetite on and off. Fishing at slack water is generally a waste of time for cod, although it may be the prime period for dabs and other 'bits' that live on the same beaches at the same time. Within an hour of the tide beginning to run, cod start moving and feeding and will continue until currents lose their momentum. Sport may slow down at the peak of a spring ebb run, which is a particularly vicious period on exposed beaches, but on the whole you can reckon that the harder the run, the faster the action will be.

Light intensity is even more critical, especially in the early days of November and during the mid-season lull. Migratory cod do not like bright light, so until darkness falls they prefer to swim well beyond casting range. Night fishing is therefore a golden rule for success. In the depths of winter, when the water is silted and the skies heavily overcast, cod move close during the day and sometimes feed quite happily. All the same, it is difficult to predict that trend and consequently the angler with only limited time at his disposal ought to hedge his bets by choosing a night tide.

Feeding Habits

During their inshore visits, cod feed almost exclusively on the sea-bed. Probably the least fussy eater in the marine world, a cod's broad philosophy is to swallow first and ask questions afterwards. Crabs, worms, fish, starfish and sea-mice, shrimps and shellfish are all recovered from the bellies of cod. As baits go, the choice is limited to those which exude a strong scent and taste. The only way that an angler can hope to attract a steady stream of cod to his tackle is by laying down a powerful scent trail, and of the dozens of baits available, only lugworm can be relied upon to draw fish consistently. Other baits do work, and some like squid are vastly superior on isolated occasions, but to rely upon them throughout the season would be stupid. Thus, the second golden rule for codding is to load the hook generously with juicy lugworms. Reinforcing and prolonging the natural scent with the biochemical attractor Biotrak is well worth the effort.

Casting Power

How far should you cast to be sure of catching cod? The pros and cons of long distance casting have been argued for twenty years at least, yet many anglers are still confused about the issue. The ability to cast a bait beyond 175 yards probably has no great bearing on a cod fisherman's overall success. Persistently blasting baits towards the horizon is as restrictive as lobbing them just

(Above) By and large, lugworm is the supreme cod bait.

(Right) Renowned for its huge cod: Chesil Beach in Dorset.

Digging lugworms for cod fishing.

Lugworm mounted on a double hook rig for extra security and better presentation.

*Piers are an ideal fishing platform when early season cod are running
beyond casting range of the beach itself.*

behind the backwash. The real advantage of learning to cast and arming
yourself with a modern beach casting outfit is to enable baits to be delivered
consistently to between 90 and 150 yards.

That the majority of cod prefer to concentrate and feed within this band is
proven beyond doubt. What remains unclear is exactly why it should be so; it
is impossible to isolate any specific current pattern, water depth or sea-bed
feature common to every beach where cod are caught. Like many angling
secrets, it is all very interesting, but in the end the main point to consider is
that to catch cod, that is where your baits must go.

(Left) The cod is a very powerful fish which eats virtually anything that comes its way.

(Below) As a rule, long casting pays off. On steep beaches like this, however, a short throw into the gutter might do the trick.

(Right) The shingle banks of East Anglia are a cod angler's paradise.

Terminal Rigs

The two priorities in cod fishing technique are to cast an attractive bait the distance necessary, and then to anchor the tackle firmly against the force of the current. Over the years, the single hook paternoster has evolved to become the standard choice. Armed with a 2/0–6/0 Spearpoint or Partridge MW hook, it will accept big baits, control heavy fish and yet be sensitive enough to detect the bite of a small codling at extreme casting range. Experienced match fishermen sometimes use a two or three hook paternoster if the sea is full of small fish, but for the all-rounder intent on taking a specimen, one heavily baited hook has a great deal to recommend it.

Other fishing books published by The Crowood Press

For further information and a copy of our latest catalogue, write to
The Crowood Press.